To the students
of Myers —

THE FRIENDSHIPS BETWEEN WOMEN

I hope this book
reminds you of

By Elaine Houston

the value
of friends!

2-06   Elaine
Houston

This book is dedicated to Msevumba

ALL LETTERS USED WITH PERMISSION OF THE AUTHOR.

All Scripture quotations from:
The Holy Bible, New International Version (NIV)
Copyright (c) 1973, 1978, 1984 by International Bible Society
Used by permission of Zondervan Publishing House

www.elainehouston.com

Cover and back photo by El-Wise Noisette
Cover design by Kim Rowan
Author's Photo by Tom Wall
Layout by Kenneth Braswell
Website Design by Kenneth Braswell

ACKNOWLEGMENTS

First of all I would like to thank God for the idea to write this book. I'd also like to thank Msevumba, a Congolese woman of great courage, for showing me about love and what it means to be committed to one's family. Many thanks to Mr. Tom Bettag and Mr. Ted Koppel of ABC Nightline for making me aware of the condition of women in Eastern Congo through their weeklong series Heart of Darkness. Thanks Mr. Bettag for corresponding with me.

Thanks also go out to my family for their support and my church family, especially the COVER GIRLS for inspiring me to believe that this project could indeed come to fruition.

THANK YOU to the powerful women who contributed letters, detailing their personal struggles and their personal victories. (I LOVE YOU) I'd also like to thank El-Wise Noisette for the fabulous cover and back photos. They captured the true essence of the Friendships Between Women. Thanks also to Cynthia Franklin the beautiful woman on the cover. Thanks to Tom Wall, who has shot publicity photos of me for 14 years and knows my "good side". Thanks to Kim Rowan. Thank you Jane Davis and Polly Hartman for your proof reading skills. Thanks to Susan Novotny for your support and our "first" meeting. Thanks Kenny Braswell and Carolyn McLaughlin for your support. Special thanks go out to Jennifer Yund and Jane Carey. Talk about the Friendships Between Women!!!!!!

This book would not have been made without the support of these two women who embraced my idea with enthusiasm. Thank you Jennifer for introducing me to Jane who always reminded me "not to worry". Thanks Boyd printing for your professionalism. Lastly, but certainly not least, a big thanks goes out to all who purchase the book. You are changing the lives of women all over the world.

Elaine Houston

Contents

INTRODUCTION

Dear _____,

My name is Elaine Houston and I want to tell you why I wrote this book.

In January 2002, I saw a story about a woman from Africa and it just broke my heart.

It was very late at night, but being the reporter that I am, as soon as I walked into the house, I immediately flipped on the television. The program "Nightline" was on and they were doing a week long series about the plight of the people in the Democratic Republic of Congo in Africa. I hadn't caught the beginning of the series, but that night I sat down with my coat still on, mesmerized by the story of Msevumba.

She was a woman in her 40's who had lost her husband to malaria after the family had been forced to run for their lives into the jungle because of war. Ruthless rebel soldiers had invaded her land and were killing, raping and looting. Women and little girls, as young as eleven, had been raped and mutilated. Looking into the faces of those women and listening to woman after woman describe what had happened to her just blew my mind. I couldn't fathom what they were saying.

Msevumba had survived with nothing but her life and now she was a father and mother to 10 kids.

To feed the family she had become a human "hauler." Stooped over she carried as much as a hundred pounds worth of other people's belongings on her back, up and down hills and mountains in the stifling heat. Sometimes she would stumble, readjust the weight on her back and start up the hill again. She did this for hours.

At the end of the day she'd be lucky to have earned 50 cents. Sometimes she would have to argue with the person who hired her just to get out of them what had been promised to her. She would spend that money to buy food, a plant of some kind, which she would then pound into powder and over a sparse fire make into a porridge. Then, she fed her children. She had so much mother wit that she knew that the dark of night was the best time to feed her beautiful babies, which she had labored for all day, because by then their little bellies would be full and they'd go off to sleep. It would be the only meal they would get in a day.

As I try to put into words and create a picture for you to show you what her life is like, I feel I'm really only showing you the negatives from a processed roll of film. The prints- I can't hand to you. Because I can't even imagine, even though I saw it with my own two eyes, what it is really like to be Msevumba. As a reporter, I've covered tornadoes, devastating fires and other tragic events and while we try our best, television can never really "put you at the scene". The scene is always more vivid, more detailed, more horrible, more beautiful, more telling.

Plain and simple her story is about violence against women. And, un- fortunately we, the world, tolerates violence against women. It's about child abuse and it's about inhumanity.

Msevumba's life is a nightmare. It is filled with unimaginable chal- lenges, and the sights of suffering few of us could ever conceive.

Yet, in the midst of it all, I managed to see this unbroken spirit, this woman who seemingly was resigned to do what ever it took to keep her kids alive and it was with that resolve that she forged ahead, using her body the way a farmer would use a field animal. Her strength made you embarrassed at how weak you are. Even with all that we have, we complain at times about having to do the laundry, shop for food or clean the house, chores that pale in comparison to what this woman had to do to exist.

The more I thought about her the madder I got.

How could such a horrible scene be playing out? Where was the out- rage? Why aren't people taking to the streets in anger? Isn't anyone else angry over this? Where are the people who will stand up and say NO! No one should have to go through THIS to live? It is inhumane!

I sat in my chair and just cried. This poor, poor woman! Every day she did this because every day her family had to eat. What a coura- geous woman, I thought.

The program had gone off and I was still sitting there thinking about Msevumba. What could I do? How could I help her? I could pray and pray to God I did. "Oh what pain she must be in. Oh, God what pain! Her feet, her back, her body, her mind, must be in so much pain. Help her Lord, Help her", I prayed.

But, the next day and the next, and months later this woman's plight was still on my mind, haunting me. Prayer was apparently not all that God wanted me to do. I had to do something else. I had seen this woman's life and now "I" was responsible for helping to make it better. So often, we see the horrible things that have befallen people, yet we just go back to our routine as if nothing had ever happened. However, I truly was my sister's keeper and I KNEW IT!

But, how could I help. What could I do? I began to think about her life and then I began to think about my own. I had had some tough times in my life and it was by the grace of God and with the help of family and friends He'd placed in my way that I had overcome them.

I started thinking about my friends and how they too had gotten through hardships in their lives with the help of other female friends. That's when the word "testimonials" came to my heart. In my church we have what we called "testimony time." A time when we would share our difficulties, and add that with the help of God we knew we would become the victor.

For me that help would sometimes come through friends who encouraged me to keep going, keep trying. Or perhaps it was someone who prayed for me or just kept tabs on me to make sure I was ok. When I was victorious, when I was free, they would also celebrate with me.

And, that is what I wanted for Mseveumba. I wanted her to know that I had seen what was happening to her and now I was calling on my friends, my sisters and we would come to her aide.

I knew that just like Msevumba there were other women either facing crises or just leaving a crisis. What if I asked these women to write letters about their own personal struggles— about how they had overcome their challenges? I also wanted them to speak of the bond of sisterhood. It would be a book full of pages addressed like letters. All the person reading would have to do is pencil in her name or the name of a woman she'd like to send the letter to. These letters she could keep and read over and over.

So, that's what I did. I also asked them to write letters about women who had inspired them, women who made life better for others and about the relationships with their sisters and mothers.

My one and only hope was that this book of letters would serve as an inspiration to all the women who read it. WOMAN, you are not alone. There are other women who have left their own personal "testimony" of survival in this book for you to read and gain strength from.

Finally, I decided I would sell the book and take the proceeds to buy food and medicine, and to create opportunities for Msevumba and the women of her village. I wanted her to never forget about The Friend-ships Between Women.

If you are reading this book right now, you are part of the never end-ing, circle of female hands that are clasped together reaching across neighborhoods, states, the United States and the world, giving sup-port to one another and gaining support from one another.

If you're going through a struggle right now and need a friend this book is for you. It doesn't matter if the struggle involves your finances, your family, your marriage, your career, your health, your emotions, your past, or the present. Like Msevumba, if there is turmoil in your country there's also a letter in here for you.

Let this book be the solvent to loosen the adhesive that's holding you back from a brighter future or the balm to soothe your wounds and encourage you to go on. Read it page by page or just read the letter that pertains to you. Then go back and read the scriptures and read them again and know that you have friends out there "clapping and shouting" for you as you cross the finish line on into victory.

Elaine Houston

THE LETTERS

Introduction to Chapter 1

Dear_____,

She's been your best friend since kindergarten. She was the one you made mud pies with and the one who came to your tea parties in the backyard. When you got your shiny new Easy Bake Oven and your new outfits for your Barbie, she's the first person you invited to your fashion show for dolls!

Wait a minute-now that I think about it, wasn't it actually in high school that the two of you met while trying to find algebra class? Soon after, it was easy pointing the two of you out walking down the hall because you were dressed like twins, same shoes, socks, pants, and blouse! Your hair was even styled the same. You talked on the phone every night. What a friendship, what a pair!

Or perhaps you met your best girlfriend in college or on the job. No matter the location or the circumstances, can you imagine life without her? Of course you can't!

That's why this first chapter celebrates FRIENDSHIP. Women's friendships are sometimes thought of as trivial, all about dresses, shoes and makeup. But as these letters will prove the Friendships Between Women are special. Our friends help us become who we were born to be. They give us hope and they help us heal.

A psychologist once told me that most women need 5 to 7 female friends. Why, because we as women have many needs. Perhaps you talk with one friend about your children, another about your career, still another inspires you and perhaps one is your traveling buddy. Have you ever noticed professional sports teams also have a core group of 5 to 7 members?

This core group keeps the game moving by feeding the ball to the others on the team and in the end it is through this team effort that the group comes out victorious. Many successful businesses also have a core group. But, whether its 1 or 7 friends you need in your life, friends are valuable and friendships are to be cherished. Find a Friend!

Elaine

Ruth 1-16

.... *But, Ruth replied don't urge me to leave or turn back from you, where you go, I will go and where you stay I will stay.*

THAT'S WHAT A FRIEND IS FOR

Dear _____,

I was getting ready for work. It was May 6th, 1988, my mom's birthday. "If I wait until tonight, I could talk to her much longer, I said to my-self".

My mom just loved to talk!

But, I'd promised to do a weave on a client and it was a time consum-ing job, especially because I couldn't get started until 6pm when she got off work.

About 4 hours into the job, the phone rang. It was my niece she said something was wrong with Big Momma. She thought she'd had a stroke.

The conversation went on, "She might be dying. They are taking her to the hospital." I was sure she was dying or dead. My mother told me she would never go to the hospital again. I was off to be with my mom the next morning at 7am.

I arrived at 11am and went directly to the hospital. Mom had requested never to be placed on life support. After much discussion the family gave in to her wishes and mother went home to be with God. I had already planned to attend a women's convention that week, it was 128 miles away from mom's home. Instead, the women I was going to the convention with came to be with me while we buried my best friend, my mom. I will always be eternally grateful to them all.

After the funeral there was much to be done. Mom lived alone and her things needed to be taken care of which meant I needed to stay at her house a while longer. One of the girls that came to the funeral told me she could stay with me. "How long, I asked."

"As long as you need me, she said."

After a week, I realized it would take much longer than I thought. My friend remained there with me for a month. She had taken time away from her family and her job to help me through the very worst time of my life. I could not have made it without her. And, I can never express enough gratitude for what she did. She knew what my mom meant to me. I thank God for my friend.

There will always be a special place in my heart for her.

Aroma Thompson

Dear _____,

Having friends is important because it makes a difference in your health, as well as your happiness.

Friends contribute to your health and add value to your life, not just because they make you feel good and help you out with problems. In studies of large populations, women with chronic diseases lived four times as long as when they had a circle of good, supportive friends, compared to women who were isolated and alone.

But friendship is not a matter of good luck, and it takes action and taking the initiative to make it happen. I learned that when I was a young adult, away from home, at my first job, I was lonesome and isolated. I spoke to a lovely little old lady, who kindly invited me to tea, and asked how I was doing. I let loose a flood of misery and complaints, and when I finished, she asked me, "My dear, have you tried to be a friend to anyone since you got here, or have you just waited for others to help you out?" Needless to say, she changed my perspective on isolation, and she helped me to become active, rather than passive. Things got a whole lot better after that.

The idea that active friend making is powerful is supported by long term research that looks at what affects the quality and length of people's lives. The Harvard Study of Adult Development, finds that the single best predictor of living a long, healthy life, is not how many people like and help you, but how many people YOU care about and support. So, it seems like the real benefit comes not so much from having friends, but rather from being a friend to others.

And that's good news, because being a friend is totally under our control. Sure, lots of people are shy or insensitive, or socially awkward, and they may not respond in a friendly way when you reach out to them. But, if you think of these folks as people who are just doing the best they can, no matter how poorly they do, then you're more likely to feel generous, rather than insulted. You can even make it a special challenge in your own mind.

Some people set goals to see how fast they can run, or how many accomplishments they can boast of, but you can set a different challenge, that is, how many "tough customers" you can make into friends. We're talking about the people who don't return your phone calls, forget your birthday, don' t appreciate what you try to do for them. They're the ones who really test our friendship abilities. But, when you keep on keeping on, you can feel pretty proud of yourself at the end of the day, no matter how somebody else behaved. And you get all the good health benefits that come from making social connections.

Dr. Lauren Ayers PhD.
Psychology

Dear_____,

I will never forget April 16, 1999. It was a Friday, the day I put my dog Samantha to sleep. It's still the hardest thing I've ever done. I felt like my heart was literally broken. The morning after, I opened my eyes and for a brief moment, it was just another day, then I remembered she was gone. I sat up, swung my legs around, my feet touched the floor and the phone rang. Just as I was about to fall apart emotionally, the very instant that I needed a friend, Vicki called. She said she was thinking about me and thought I might need to talk. The tears just came, fast and furious, partly because I missed Sammy and partly because I felt God sent Vicki. He knew I needed someone and there she was at the very second I was falling apart.

Vicki and I work together and there have been so many other times when she has just called or walked over to my desk, simply noticing when I am in need. She doesn't make a big deal out of it, just quietly lets me know she's there to help.

I remember, one day, I was so stressed. It seemed as if everything was going wrong. I felt like I was going to snap and say things I didn't want to say. An hour or so passed, I can't even remember exactly how much time it was, but it was enough for Vicki to take a lunch break or something. When she returned, she secretly placed a card on my keyboard. It was one of those "hang in there" cards. She wrote her own message just to let me know that she saw I was struggling, she cared, and if she could help she wanted to.

It is as if whenever I'm in need, Vicki's there, offering friendship. She heals my heart. She's an answer to my prayers. I want to live my faith. I want to be Christ to others. I want people to see Him in my actions, my words, my eyes and my smile. It's real hard at work. I pray for strength there and I believe Vicki's an answer to prayer. I'm not sure if she even believes in God, but He works through her for me. She is truly an angel in my life and I feel blessed by her friendship.

Kathy Barrans

Dear _____,

Almost six years ago, when I was diagnosed with metastasis breast cancer, there was an incredible outpouring of support from my many friends in the NY Women's Bar Association, which I will never forget.

Judge Leslie Stein was by my side at the biopsy when I received the news. Pat Martinelli rushed over to my house that evening with an armful of breast cancer books and with the wisdom born of her own experience with the disease. Mara Ginsberg, whose organization To Life! has helped so many breast cancer patients, personally guided me through treatment options and all the ancillary details (wigs, etc.) that are so important in maintaining dignity during the process. Judge Beverly Tobin also reached out to me to share her personal experience and to offer her encouragement.

Friends too numerous to mention by name showered me with cards and flowers, some even sending hot, homemade meals so that I wouldn't have to cook following surgery. But, what touched me the most was a single card from the Women's Bar Board of Directors containing the names of almost two dozen members who wanted to drive me to weekly chemo treatments (even though it meant taking off more than half a day of work). Sitting in a chair for two hours while they pump nauseating poison into your veins was not something to look forward to, but the treatments seemed to fly by with the companionship of these strong, upbeat women telling me jokes, sharing stories and just holding my hand.

I am convinced that the support of these amazing women made all the difference in my recovery and I might not be writing this letter without them.

Rachel Kretser

Dear_____,

I am often reminded of my spiritual guidance through a dear friend by the name of Grace. Although she cannot account for my soul salvation, she sure has been a great asset to my life.

People are only complete when they have a true friend to understand them, to share all their passions, sorrows, and to stand by them throughout their lives.

Grace, you are someone who is concerned with everything I do.

Grace, you are someone I call upon during good and bad times.

Grace, you are someone who understands the things I may do.

Grace, you always tell me the truth about myself.

Grace, you always know what I am doing at all times.

Grace, you never try to compete with me.

Grace, you are genuine about being happy when things are going well.

Grace, you are an extension of myself, and without you as a true friend my life would not be complete.

Love always,

Selena

Dear_____,

My best friend growing up was and currently is an amazing woman. She was like the sky in my world, always with me day and night. There is a story about the sky, by Richard Bach, and when we were away from each other during a long summer, she recorded that story for me on a tape and sent it to me.

The comfort of the story was a welcome relief and in hearing her voice, the beginning of school did not seem so far away. She seemed to understand what I needed at just that time. Without talking to me about it, or writing to inquire how I was doing, she recorded the story and sent it to me, and instantly, the sun seemed to break through into my cloudy world. I don't think she knows how much I ever truly appreciated that small gesture, and how many days, that short story lingers with me and the sun is shining.

She has been through hard times herself, and to this day, we seem to have this unspoken bond and wavelength. One of us is always able to hone in on the other one, realizing when we are needed. My friend and I are like the skies. We shift and change through sun and storm. Yet, having the sky surrounding me brings me a personal sense of security, love and comfort. Do we ever outgrow those friendships? Ever feel like as adults we have flushed out those two inseparable little girls? Often I feel that way, then the clouds clear and the sun streams through and with a smile I know she is still with me. She has played a large part in the person that I have become, having taken on some of her strongest characteristics and adopting them into who I am. We are two completely separate people who have shared a lifetime full of shared memories.

Kathylynn Bentz

Dear_____,

I'm writing this letter to let you know that I consider you a true friend. Yes, many people have said it, many times, but I want you to know why I consider you my FRIEND.

You are a person with a big heart. Whenever I needed comfort, whether in word or deed, it was you who was there for me.

I remember when I needed to leave an abusive husband you were there for me. I remember that you wouldn't come into the house, but you gave me transportation to my parent's house.

You never said, "Leave him." You were there for me.

When I was struggling to pay bills and couldn't afford to buy my daughter Christmas presents, you bought her a coat for Christmas, and for that I will always be thankful. You never looked for anything in return because you did it from the heart.

When my daughter had surgery, not once but twice, you were there with me at the hospital. As a matter of fact you stayed with her, while I ran errands.

I thank you for all the friendship cards you sent over the years. They truly let me know that you are my best friend.

Last but not least, when my mother died, you were with me when I had to collect her belongings and you cooked meals so I didn't have to.

One of the definitions for friend is confidant. It signifies a closeness that words cannot describe. We've shared a great deal over the years. You are a person I can trust.

You are a friend that sticks closer than a brother. God could not have blessed me with a better friend than you.

Your Good Buddy,

Marcia

Dear _____,

You don't know how it happens or when it gets started, but you know the special lift it always brings. And you realize that Friendship is God's most precious gift!

Friends are a very rare jewel, indeed. They make you smile and encourage you to succeed. They lend an ear, they share a word of praise, and they always want to open their hearts to us.

Author unknown

The passage above expresses my sentiments regarding 'my friend'. I've known my friend for over 20 years and our friendship has increasingly become much richer and fulfilling.
While I knew my friend for some time before a friendship developed, it wasn't until the 80's that we actually connected in a meaningful way.

We've encountered many tests and trials along the way. People have misunderstood our relationship from the beginning and have tried unsuccessfully to break it up. We've stood the test of time. Praise God!

Most of our communicating is done via telephone and e-mails. We rarely see each other socially or otherwise.

However, we remain connected. There have been times (not very often) when she or I would get a whiff of a slight disconnection brewing. We do not let it linger however. We'd promptly make plans to get together and we'd talk about whatever has caused the disconnections. Immediately, the sweet smell of friendship would fill the air again.

Once, when our children were younger, we shared bread, yes slices of bread so our children could have a sandwich for lunch. That's how my friend and I are, like a sandwich, peanut butter and jelly to be exact, because we blend together so well. I don't know how it happened or when it started, I'm just glad it did.

Joyce Brown

Dear_____,

A friend is a person who loves you and will never bring up your faults. They will hold the things you tell them and will weigh it against who they know you are, discard what is not good and hold the rest until you want to talk about it. They will not judge you before you are ready and then they only have suggestions for you to change. They are good listeners and if they give any criticism, it does not feel negative. No one is a true friend, until they can hear all the good, bad and in between and still love you.

They have to spend time with you, share your dreams and see you in good times and in bad times. In this life if you have one friend like this, you are blessed. It is a rare thing to have a true friend with no jealousy, no envying and no competition. I have been fortunate to have such a person in my life. I have had my friend now for 22 years. With all we have been through only death will part us, and then the memories will continue for the one left behind.

We both love to shop and sometimes we shop for nothing at all, it is really so we can be together. We just love being together. We just hang out, walking in and out of the stores cutting up, trying on this and that for no good reason. We buy each other things on no special occasion, just to say, "I love you girl". We walk around holding hands and then laugh because we know that people are staring and we know what they are thinking, but we don't care.

I remember when I started graduate school. This is funny now but it was not so funny then. As we did everyday, sometimes twice a day, I called her almost in tears. "Girl, I don't know what I think I am doing going to school at my age. That teacher wants me to write a paper on the color BLUE!

Now, what am I going to say about blue? Except the sky is blue" Well, we had a good laugh about that and she listened to me read my paper for the next couple of days until I turned it in. To our surprise, the instructor thought it had potential and gave it back to me for a few corrections.

We fell out laughing (over the phone) and I continued going to school and writing papers, until one day to her surprise I said, "This paper writing is so easy, as long as you do an outline and have your stuff organized it's a breeze." Well, that surprised me too, but all along she had more faith in me than I did. She was such an encouragement to me— and that continued through graduate school. (She should have gotten a degree too for all she had to put up with.) That was reason for celebration but we celebrated life in general. Those celebrations could be as simple as a card with words that were so meaningful. Or one of our shopping trips. Nothing big, as long as we were together, we were happy. I will always love my friend. If people had marriages like our friendship there would be no divorces.

Trudy Lawson

Dear_____,

A friend is someone who lets their actions speak louder than their words. Over the years, you have been a good friend and our friend-ship has been tested time after time, but we overcame those tests. We are still friends to this day. Thank you so much for being my friend. I remember the time you volunteered to share your home with my family for a night, even though there were seven people in your family! We cooked a big meal, the children played and we had a good time.

A friend is someone to have fun with. I remember all the things we've shared together over the years, all the fun and laughs. Remember the night we were asked by the fellas to play strip poker and you ran and put on six layers of clothing under your coat!!   What a laugh we all had.

I also remember the sad times and the times of sorrow we shared. I have wiped your tears and held your hands and I was glad that it gave you comfort.

When I think of our times together I sit back and grin, girl, we've been through thick and thin!   Thanks "M" for being my friend.

L.F.

Dear_____,

I am the mother of three children. You're probably saying to yourself, "That's a handful". And, you probably can't believe I would increase my responsibilities by taking on two more children. But, I did!

Soon after we took them in, my friend started to bless me with practically everything the two girls needed to wear. From tops to bottoms, she gave us wonderful things that I could never afford. She continued to do this until they graduated from high school.

But her generosity didn't stop there, not only did she clothe them physically, but she clothed them emotionally by always encouraging them to do well. Often she encouraged me too, inspiring me to "keep on keeping on" and bringing me a little gift. She gave me so much support in so many ways. I will always be grateful for her friendship and the help she has given to me. She is truly a great friend.

Aroma Thompson

Dear _____,

I'm writing to tell you about my very best friend, Lela. Lela and I met in the summer of 1991, both of us enrolled in the same Lamaze class. I was expecting my second child. Lela, her first.

It was a brutally hot summer that year. Lela and I suffered through it, knowing that we would be forever changed at the end of this journey.

Lela's son was born on September 1st. The very next day my daughter was born. The experience of motherhood is like an emotional roller coaster, exhilaration mixed with worry, delight mixed with anxiety. Everyone questions their ability as a parent, am I doing too much, too little, what if (you fill in the blank) happens? And of course, when will I ever get a good night's sleep again? Lela and I became fast friends as we struggled through those first tiring weeks.

Lela has always been a true friend. That doesn't mean we agree on everything! Lela's always been there when I've needed a shoulder to cry on. When my life was turned upside down she was my anchor. When I needed to reinvent myself as a single mother and reconstruct my world, Lela was compassionate and honest. She didn't tell me what I wanted to hear. She told me what I needed to hear, so that I could begin rebuilding my life. She was there to encourage me when I decided to start my own business. Ever since that first hot summer day when we first met, Lela's been there to support, encourage, critique, argue, laugh and cry. We're more like sisters than most sisters I know.

Everyone should be as fortunate as I have been! Lela is a gift that becomes more precious with time. I know I was blessed when our paths first crossed, way back in the summer of 1991.

Sincerely,

Kathleen Godfrey

Dear _____,

Some friends are there to give you a hug, a smile, or a shoulder to cry on. My friends give me unconditional availability. They are always there when I need them. Here's my story.

My friends and I don't live near each other. Like a lot of people these days, some of us have moved away from our hometown.

So, now miles separate our friendship. Recently an event brought us all back together emotionally as well as physically.

We were asked to be bridesmaids (and bow person) in another friend's wedding. Immediately, we began planning a shower, putting together ideas and a possible location. By the first of the year (the shower was to be in August) we had everything set, an event worthy of a queen. All we needed was a guest list. All of us were very excited and were already anticipating the surprise, joy, and tears of emotion as the bride to be arrived at her surprise shower.

With everyone's spirits high we received a guest list with well over a hundred people on it! To say the least it shocked us a bit. Some people don't have weddings that big! We needed to cut the list for our plans to come to fruition for we had a budget to meet. Subsequently many unpleasant things began to happen and snowballed from there.

The bride now began to get involved with the shower. She said some unkind things to the six of us planning the shower, which left us hurt and insulted.

I won't go into a lot of detail, for this story is not the point, the point is that the event triggered a bond between the six of us that nothing, not even a shower gone haywire could destroy.

But, it also did something else. It allowed us to put into action the definition of friendship. Although, a monkey wrench had been thrown into what was supposed to be a tribute from us to our friend (the bride) and a truly blessed day for her, we showed what kind of friends we were and continued working on the shower. And we pulled it off!

In fact, we, the planners, came out of this with an even bigger appreciation for the friendships we have with one another.

This event was an eye opener for me. The real things in life are love, laughter, a family that loves you and friends that will always be there for you.

To the bride I say those are the real things in life, not the material things. To my friends, I say thank you! You are all sisters from God. I just want you to know how much I appreciate you and this gang I belong to, for knowing you are in my life I will never be lonely.

Love you always. God bless you.

Lori

Dear_____,

After attending a wedding, I went window-shopping with a couple of friends. I had a great day. Just before bedtime I developed a headache and became quite ill.

I ended up having to be hospitalized for five weeks.

My friend, who I've known for about ten years, showed me what a true friend she really was.

She came to the hospital every day. She did everything she could to make me as comfortable as she possibly could.

She used her experience as a nurse's aide and every other skill she had to help me recuperate.
She rubbed my back, made my bed, and combed my hair. When the hospital's linen caused me to itch she made comfortable bed pads to place under me. She kept in contact with my husband and children, washed my gowns and after I came home, she was there caring for me until I was on my feet again, which was about a year later. What a true, life long friend she turned out to be. I will be forever grateful to her for being there for me during a very tough time. I love her.

Aroma Thompson

Dear_____,

Hey there, lonely girl, where's your girlfriend? I can't imagine myself without a "girl" friend. At least one! Without a friend, whom do you share your accomplishments with?

Who do you tell your little secrets, those little dreams or goals or plans that are a ways off but possible, difficult but thrilling at the same time.

Who do your tell your BIG DREAMS to? DREAMS SO BIG, that at first, you hesitate saying them aloud, for fear people would laugh.

Who prays for you? Who prays with you?

Who do you talk to about what you wish love would be like if love came knocking at your door?
What about the latest Mr. Right? Only, a true friend would tell you he's really Mr. Wrong and that you deserve so much better than that!!

Who do you brag to about your kids?

Or ANNOUCE to 'I WANT TO HAVE A BABY or I'm gonna get me a cat!!!

What about those "crazy" ideas of yours, like running for political office or a marathon, or losing 100 pounds. Would a friend say those are crazy ideas and try to talk you out of them?

Remember when you wanted to learn to swim, and ride a bike, and play the piano and tap dance and roller blade, things you should have done as a child or at summer camp but didn't and now you want to try as an adult! Who listened to that litany of lost youth and didn't snicker until you finished spilling it and then laughed so hard, you both doubled over?

A friend is a person who always wants the best for you, who will tell you the truth when you need to be told.

A friend will notice that you've put on a few pounds and then go shopping with you to help you find that all over "panty girdle thingy" that is advertised to suck in your stomach like a vacuum sucks up dirt.

A friends cries with you when you lose your diamond and squeals when you finally get that "rock" from your beloved.

Like Ruth, in the scripture above, a friend won't leave you when you've lost it all or taken the biggest blow of your life.

According to Prevention Magazine, a female researcher, studying the effects of friendship on cancer growth, discovered that higher levels of social well being were associated with lower levels of a cancer promoting substance known as vascular endothelial growth factor. In a nutshell, having friends may help fight cancer growth.

Another study, done at UCLA, suggests that when we associate with female friends, a chemical in the brain is released that counters stress and produces a calming effect. This calming effect apparently does not occur in men.

So how much more evidence do you need before you give friendship a try?

What's that you say, you've tried the 'friendship thing' and had your feelings hurt or maybe even your heart broken.

I know what you mean; I've been there too. But, sometimes finding a "true" friend is like buying a pair of shoes; you have to try on a few pairs before you find one with a good fit.

Once, a friend said to me, friends come into your life for a reason, a season or forever. And, maybe that person you thought was a friend fits into one of those categories. The most important thing is that you don't give up on friendship, because the right friend will expand and enrich your life in ways you never imagined. Get out there and try it again "friendless." First, show yourself friendly; you get back what you give out. Then, try the person on for size, be honest, be true and look for the same in return. Before you know it, you'll be laughing until your side hurts and shopping in the mall until your feet hurt, but it will be worth it because you're doing it with your friend.

Elaine Houston

Chapter Reflections

Introduction to Chapter 2

Dear_____,

I love this chapter! I love stories where the underdog wins!!!!!!!!! I love to see victory grab defeat by the neck and squeeze all the life out of it. When you read letters like "Hard pressed on every Side," you'll see what I mean.

"Dear Survivor" will show you no matter how you came into the world, when it comes to God's plan for your life you will win!   These letters are evidence that we as women may go through divorce, illness, betrayal, oppression, rejection, heart-ache, abuse, loneliness, you name it, but we will win! And, along the way there are other women standing on the side-lines, like spectators watching a marathon, cheering us on to victory. They can do this because they've been equipped with strength, learned about survival and have been filled with compassion while going through their own valley experience.

Girl, if I can make it through this, you can too!

Elaine

Romans 8-37

.... No, in all these things we are more than conquerors.

Girl, If I Can Get Through This, You Can Too!

Dear_____,

I know there are times when you feel you will never get through this trial. There's just too much that needs to be straightened out before you will feel better and be better. How can everything be messed up at once? All hell is breaking loose in your home, with your extended family and friends, your finances, your health, your job and even in your church. You know God is there. You haven't left Him or your covenant walk with Our Father. Sometimes your heart actually hurts and you have chest pains. You may say what have I done or not done to deserve all of this.

In order to encourage you I will have to share my wounds. Just thinking about that time in my life makes tears come to my eyes. I felt like there was a boulder on my back even though I knew that one of the promises of God is that He will not put more on you than you can bear. Everything does happen for a reason. And God will get the glory out of our lives, if we allow Him to guide us through the storms.

Have you ever been in a car wash? The brushes are spinning— soap and water are thrown at you. It is a very violent time. Once, I was in the car wash and all the machines stopped. What should I do? Get out and run back to the booth. Yes, that's what I'll do. Just as I was about to open the car door, the machine started up. What if I had gotten out?

That's when God gave me the illustration of the trials I was going through. Stay in the safety of the Lord. My husband had left me for probably the third time (we separated so many times, I honestly can't recall the number) in February 1996.

I was in a car accident that totaled my car in September 1996. I was injured and needed surgery, which I put off until August 2002-never a good time to be out of work and on disability.

Just when I started to accept the situation I was told I must leave the only house my children have ever known as home. I had rented this home for 13 years. (I could have owned a home with the money I paid my landlord) Now, the state had decided to build a post office on the very spot I called home. Without the love and support of friends, my children and I would have been homeless. To be honest, we did not have a home of our own so we were homeless.

In February of 1998, my sister Cynthia was diagnosed with breast

46

cancer. In August 1998, my divorce became final. My sister was 39 years old. We are eleven months apart. I mean we were eleven months a part. Yes, God took her to be with Him June 19th, 1999, Father's Day. In March 2000, my father was in a car accident that leaves a man dead. In August of that same year, my daughter Kirstin was diagnosed with a kidney disorder that was very serious. I never lost faith. I did lose hope. But God was there through it all. During that period of my life I felt like I would never be happy again. But, I stayed with God and He stayed with me. I want you to know you can make it. You will make it. You may be hard pressed on every side but you are not nor will you be crushed. Keep praying. Keep fasting. Keep believing.

Looking back, I know had I not leaned on God I have no idea where I would be. Be encouraged. You too will arrive on the other side. Just stay in the boat.

Your sister in Christ,

Cheryl A. Scott

Dear_____

It is hard to believe that 17 years have passed since we held each other in a long embrace. With tears streaming down your face and a heart heavy with the pain of loss, you mourned the departure of a sister to a faraway land, a sister who shared every moment of your life. You knew it was a defining moment. Fate has parted our paths and separated our future with vast oceans. My excitement with the new life that awaited me clouded my vision and suppressed my tears. Little did I know where the journey would take me and little did I know what I would lose along the way.

I sailed to shores of the unknown. Setting foot on land, I realized that my right to define who I am was no longer mine. Little by little it became clear to me that my predicament was to relentlessly strive to prove that I did not fit their definition of what women in my culture feel, act, think and behave.

Everywhere I went labels followed me. They haunted my days and nights. I tried to ignore them, laugh at them, rebel against them, fight them but repeatedly succumbed to their tangled web. For the plight of Arab women, who live in a society that demonizes their culture and defines them with the label of oppression, violence and ignorance is to constantly struggle to remove the label or to internalize the definitions and resign to their crushing weight.
No matter which path they choose, they will realize they will never be Home again.

So, I turned to the struggle. I realized that to snatch back any power of self-definition, I must not rest. I climbed the ladder of higher education to the top to remove the label "uneducated". I founded my family life on the principles of justice, fairness and equality to remove the label "oppressed." I worked relentlessly day and night to remove the label "unproductive." I refused to mask over signs of premature aging that crept up on me with incredible speed to prove I am not "frivolous." I suppressed my feminine attributes to prove I am not an object for someone's enjoyment. I studied the culture of my new adopted land to understand its frame of mind and its history. It's a constant struggle to stay afloat, amid formidable tides of prejudice.

Almost every first encounter brings feelings of frustration and anger. The same cold looks, same attitudes that doubt your capability, that question your worth, reduce your humanity to a mere half or less, that act on fictitious conjured up assumptions of "poor" downtrodden" "uneducated" oppressed." They never cease to send shivers down my spine, darken my days, haunt my nights, and shackle my tongue.

Private encounters are not the only source of emotional and mental assault on my Arab identity.
The demonizing of Arabs and their culture is a public affair that is approved, blessed and nurtured by the dominant society. I often wonder what if the word "Muslim" or "Arab" were substituted for the word "Black" or "Jewish" or "Mormon?" Many people would have lost their jobs, and countless others would have scrambled for public apologies.

Will we ever see the dawn of a day when Arabs will be a minority group, granted the same public respect and right of dignity as other minorities. When will we as Arabs stop being forced to carry the burden of guilt and a stigma for crimes we have not committed, for crimes we have denounced publicly and privately? When will we be treated as innocent until proven guilty? Will we ever be given the chance to feel home?

While it seems at times that the one thing America agrees on is the need for an aggressive, all out mental assault on Arab culture and identity, there are some angles of hope who swim against the tide, carrying a flickering light amid the darkness. Their conscience rejects oppression as a matter of principle and renounces all its manifestation. While their voices are being drowned and silenced, their mere existence keeps blood flowing in my veins.

I desperately tried to fill the void you left in my life.

I gathered all the memories of our childhood and placed them in a sacred place. In it, I stored our dreams, aspirations, fears, laughter, and the endless stories we shared at bedtime about the people we encountered in our days.

I stored images of the Guava trees we constantly climbed and the "pond" we dug in the garden. I stored images of you fighting back sleep to "help" me study for my college entry exams. I stored our celebrations of the milestones in our lives. Our belief in who we are and our disappointments and frustrations at our human limitations that we thought did not exist. I stored a memory of a time shared, free of the burdens of adulthood.

I gathered all the pieces of our childhood and harnessed the energy they emanated to dissolve the anger within, an anger that kept wrapping its web tightly around me.

It became clear to me only then will I be able to rise above the clouds and embrace the possibilities that lie beyond. I realize how the anger that I harbored had widened the chasm between myself and the rest of human kind, how it had slowly and painfully stripped me of the energy to fight, resist and struggle to maintain who I am, and to convey my self-definitions to whomever I encountered. The less anger I had, the more positive human connections I was able to establish and the more able I was to be a self-definer. Every victory strengthens my resolve to continue the journey. Every milestone feeds my determination to push ahead for more victories. I will never be alone again, and one day I will be Home.

Forever,

Dina

Dear_____,

My daughter was diagnosed with breast cancer, which was aggressive and spreading fast. I was numb after getting the news. I realize now that God had caused me not to absorb the news in a way that would be devastating to me. I went into a somber but prayerful mode.

 I called friends who were people of prayer and solicited their comfort and encouragement. Throughout the months of treatment I remained prayerful and hopeful.

The dismal prognosis of 18 months to live was seven years ago. God continues to heal my daughter. She is alive and her last physical attests to God's miracle working power. All the test results were normal. All glory and honor to God.

Enid Arthur

Dear_____,

When the odds were against me the Almighty God blessed me. I was born out of wedlock and against my mother's will. She gave birth to me even before she could enjoy being a teenager. Her trauma had a devastating effect on me as well. I was physically and emotionally abused. In spite of the odds, I was blessed to have beautiful grand-mothers and an aunt who loved me.

These women looked after me and showered me with agape love. My maternal grandmother provided for me. She had a second grade edu-cation but inspired me to get MY education. She knew how much I loved clothes and said "Baby as long as you stay in school I will supply you with a wardrobe." Even after I kept my part of the deal and had graduated with my first Masters Degree, raised two sons and gotten divorced she still bought me things. I thank God for her.

As a child, my great grandmother was very spiritual and prayerful. I will never forget that when my young life was filled with turmoil she made it a point to take me to church every Sunday. Church was a spiritual hospital, a place where I could take refuge.

My paternal grandmother took an active role in my life when I was a teen. When I needed something new and invigorating to preoccupy my time she got me involved in cotillions and beauty pageants.

I wasn't much older than my dear Great aunt, yet she tried to teach me everything.

She embraced me as though I was her biological daughter. When she went away to college, I was in middle school. Once a month, she would invite me to visit her on campus for the weekend. During my young life I did not know how to really appreciate these beautiful women but today I thank God for them and will never forget "these bridges" that carried me over.

Just as it took four people to raise me, I have had to call on others to help me raise my children after my first marriage of 17 years ended. Those helpers included my church family, friends, and co-workers. Education and a strong work ethic were messages that I imparted into my kids. It has not been easy for my young men, the separation, the divorce and three open-heart surgeries for my oldest son. It has not been easy for me either. There were times when I thought I was going to lose it. I've had many tests in my life. I did not dot every 'I" and cross every "T" but, I know there is a God and he has truly smiled on me. Having faith and perseverance, I was determined to achieve. I am blessed to have earned two Masters Degrees, numerous awards and I'm currently working on a doctorate degree. My eldest son is a senior in college and my youngest is a college junior.

Finally, I do not think of myself as better than anyone else and if the Lord brought me through he can do it for you. It just takes a willing spirit.

Shilene Moultrie-Johnson

Dear_____,

I am proud to be one of many women around the globe taking a stand to appreciate what we, as women, can achieve, if only we chose to make a difference.

5 years ago, I met one of your sisters in this action in my hometown of Kigali-Rwanda. Her name is Wendy Cue. She was working for the United Nations Human Rights division. When Wendy found out that I was a genocide survivor, she was interested in learning what had really happened in the country and how a few of us survived. This was 4 years after the genocide that killed over a 1,000,000 unarmed, innocent civilian men, women, and children. They died because they were born Tusti, a minority group in my country. Their neighbors, friends, and relatives hacked them down. Wiping tears from my eyes, I told her the following story:

During this tragedy, I lost most of my family members. Jean Damascene (my husband) and all his family, Felicien (my father), Agnes (my sister), Gervais (my uncle), Antoinette (my aunt) and her disabled child, Esperance, (my cousin) and her newborn baby boy, and many other extended family members. Under normal circumstances, when you lose your family, close friends take you in as one of their own family members. Unfortunately, my close friends didn't survive either.

I was eight months pregnant when the genocide started. After giving away all our belongings to the militia gangs who were sent to kill both my husband and me, we decided to seek refuge at a longtime Hutu friend. But, he threw us out of his home, claiming he had nothing to do with Tusti's anymore. We spent the first night in a nearby classroom, sitting on a freezing, dirty cement floor. The following day, a Good Samaritan family agreed to help me. My husband also found refuge but in a different home. I never saw him again after that.

After many weeks, days and nights, of hiding under the children's bed of the family that took me in, the militia found me and took me to the local public administration officer who was a mother of seven children. Her daughter begged her mother to save my life, and she did. For the next few weeks, I lived in the home of this public administration officer who was also the local coordinator of the genocide!

While she was protecting me in her home, she also carried out her duties of actively participating in the killings of thousands of people in her district. On the night of May 8th, 1994, I gave birth to my baby girl

54

in a wet small house behind the kitchen house in this woman's back-yard. It was raining heavily and I was all alone in there. The next morning, I was found exhausted by the Interahamwe (those who attack together) and taken to the "butchery" site. That morning, I didn't look good enough for a good machete cut. They made me wait for a "better looking" victim who would go first.

Meanwhile, in a nearby home, there was a pile of various items stolen from homes whose owners had been killed, and from a nearby school and shops.

Most of them were electrical items that looters had little knowledge of their use.

While they were still waiting for a new victim to be brought to the "butchery site" they took me to this house to help them sort out the stock. They had guns and my wish was that I could ask them to shoot me and my child instead of using the machetes to kill us, shooting would have been quicker, but I did not have money to pay them for a gun shot and a quicker way of dying.

Once they realized that they had kitchen equipment in this house, they decided to keep me alive as long as I could cook for them. It was important for the killers to make sure that all eyewitnesses of their inhumane actions are all killed, as advised by their senior genocide planners.

Miraculously, when the Rwanda Patriotic Army took the city, the militia were not at the house and the security guard hired to guard the house and make sure that I did not escape, didn't have a key to the house or a hand grenade to blow it up. He ran away to save his own life and left us alive.

After I told my story to Wendy, she decided to make a difference in my life. She shared her intentions with her friends. With great responsibilities waiting ahead, further education was a priority for me.

While searching for schools with a curriculum geared towards social work, I found the College of St. Rose. It caught my attention simply because my daughter's name is Rose de Mystica. Coincidentally, this school was located in Wendy's hometown of Albany, NY. Wendy connected me to her best friend's parents Ken and Marggie Skinner. I will never forget the day I got their first e-mail offering my daughter and me a room in their home. We arrived in Albany on December 30th, 2001. I feel blessed to be able to work towards my dreams. But, I also carry a new dream with me, which is to keep the "make a differ-ence" lights alive.

Every time I look at Ken and Marggie, I wonder how many people can do as much as they have done for someone they never met. May God bless them and many of you with whom I share the belief that there are endless opportunities to make a difference in someone else's life.

Eugenie Mukeshimana

Dear_____,

If I were to address this letter to someone's attention I would address it "Dear Lost Soul." Here's my story. I was born in 1961 on a cold November day. I weighed 3 pounds and four ounces. My fight for survival had begun.

I was the product of a compulsory marriage and as a result saw first-hand the discontentment, disappointment, and torment that comes out of a marriage of convenience, a marriage created to solve the problem of youthful, uninformed sexual encounters.

My father was my sun, moon and stars, so when he and my mother split I was devastated. We moved away from our home and friends to my grandmother's home and my father was looked upon as the enemy.

The years at my grandmother's house left many scars. During that time my childhood ended in so many ways. And, the saddest feelings I had were the feelings of worthlessness. This worthlessness filled my summer days and somehow the cold, sticky sweetness of a melting ice cream cone brought minimal pleasure.

During this period I had my first encounter with "an edge." I climbed an apple tree and stood at the edge of a large branch and being six years old the distance down seemed endless. That was the first time I thought of death, of endings, of overwhelming desolation, of misunderstood violations and of broken trusts.

My mother married again. My stepfather gave the impression that he would have preferred a wife without children, especially two black children. We became children who were seen and not heard. If we voiced displeasure over mistreatment we were labeled as disrespectful and ungrateful.

We moved from granny's house to a large, new house with a pool. There was a new car every year and what appeared to be all any child would ever want or need.

We'd stepped up the social ladder but then the fighting started. It was no surprise to anyone. The marriage was based on passion and necessity. The wars began and this is where I made my exit.

I stayed away as much as possible, filling my emotional void with cloudy dreams that I thought only weed, pills, LSD or cocaine could provide. I also experienced my first consensual sexual encounter.

In the fall of 1979, I went to the Fashion Institute of Technology. My parents never flinched when their 16 year-old daughter got on a bus to New York City. The city amazed me; the lights, the people and the excitement. I found the school work easy and bloomed from a chubby country girl to a slim model in no time. This transformation changed my self image and I became a confident, attractive, young woman. My grades were good and I was earning money modeling and dating several cute guys. Then my world was shattered when I was sexually assaulted and left bleeding in a parking garage near school.

As I took a shower, all the glamour and my self confidence ran down the drain. I made only one phone call and that was to obtain heroin. I felt it was the only thing that would wash away the terrible agony permeating through my desperate mind, heart and shattered soul.

I thought of drugs like an old friend I'd come to rely on to dull the pain no matter how great.

Years passed, one broken marriage, one child. And 20 years later, I woke up in an intensive care unit, after a suicide attempt. My world was falling apart. I had been indicted for conspiracy to sell cocaine. I had lost my credibility at the New York State Assembly. I was estranged from my child and my family and worst I could no longer hide behind the haze. All the pain I'd buried deep inside and medicated with drugs came rushing back. No amount of drugs held back the torrent of emotions.

I was sent to an adult treatment facility for 14 months. I was a frightened and broken 38 year old woman with an emotional mentality of a 9 year old. I realized I had no answers.

Even though I'd survived many years on my own I had to surrender myself completely to the idea that I was not in control and had no answers. This surrender allowed me, for the first time, to hear that I could hope for a life where I no longer felt like the stranger, where I no longer lived on the cusp of society and kept up appearances for the sake of others, where I could come to realize that the opinion others have of me is not as vital as the opinion I have of myself.

Thanks to the help of Charlene and Cheryl at the Hope House Adult Treatment facility in Albany, NY, I have come away whole. I am clean and still diligently working on my mental health issue. And, I'm pleased to say that the cold, sticky sweetness of an ice cream cone melting on a warm summers day is just that sweet.

So, to my lost friend, I hope this letter helps you realize that though the details of our stories may differ, the pain and sorrow are very much the same. I feel strongly that it is only when we embrace ourselves, respect ourselves and love ourselves, that we will know peace.

With Sincerity,

Carla Ellis

Dear_____,

My journey in life began on September 12, 1950. I was a change of life child born to middle age parents and into a middle class Jewish family. I was nine months of age when my father died of a heart attack. It was then that the saga of Nadine Robin began to unfold.

Taking on the roles of both parents, my mother handed me the world at my feet and placed me on a pedestal. Unbeknownst to her, the expectations and aspirations she had for me would be my "Achilles heel."

Materialistically, I wanted for nothing but emotionally my shell was packed with low self-esteem, no self worth, hopelessness, the need to be needed, etc. My mother could only show her love through what she could buy me (jewelry, clothes, cars and trips to Europe). I never got hugs, kisses, compliments or words of encouragement. I thought the way to show love was by "buying".

To fill these voids, I turned to men, drugs, crime and so on and so forth. My choices were like a row of dominoes with a tumbling effect. My losses were insurmountable and my "highs" consisted of that feeling of numbness that you get from drugs. During this leg of my journey, I lost my mother, my professional standing, myself, my freedom. I ended up in a Federal Prison Camp in Danbury, Connecticut.

It was at this point in my life at 45 years of age that Joanne and Charlene became a part of my "rebirth". Joanne was my Federal Probation Officer and Charlene was my Counselor at Hope House Residential Treatment Facility for Substance Abuse. These two women saw in me what I could not see in myself. Joanne sent me to Hope House instead of back to Danbury Federal Prison Camp when I was continually using drugs again. It was at the age of 45 that I grew up. I was so used to controlling my own destiny that I did not think anyone needed to help me. Never would I ask for help. I carried the world on my shoulder and thought I could solve all of my problems.

I never put myself first. I took care of everyone and everything. Charlene through her counseling approach made me look at and learn about myself. She encouraged me to reveal my innermost fears, feelings and reach for the stars.

Had Joanne not sent me to Hope House for treatment, I would not be standing on solid ground. She gave me the door to my future and

Charlene taught me the steps that allowed me to open the door and walk on through.

Without, these two supportive women, I would not be where I am today. I have eight years and five months of sobriety, am property manager for a federally–funded Housing Authority and more importantly, I am a woman who is proud of her accomplishments. I have learned that it is never too late, never say never, you are never alone, never give up hope and I am worthwhile.

Today, I can look in the mirror and like the woman who is looking back at me.

With hope and love,

Nadine

Dear_____,

I am a survivor of a stalker.

In 1997 I ended a two and a half year relationship with a man I thought I knew and trusted. I assisted the police after he vandalized merchandise in an antique center. He was eventually arrested and paid restitution. He blamed me for his situation and began harassing me at work and at home. I was a teacher at the time and he called my superintendent, principals in the district and the state Education Department of Teacher Discipline. He continually told these people that I had encouraged him to commit the crime and since I taught children I should be fired. But, because I had a stellar thirty-year reputation in my school district his allegations were not believed.

So, he then began harassing me by phone. At its worst I was receiving over 70 hang-ups a day. Using my telephone was difficult as he always tied up the line. I had to unplug my phone at night so I could shut out the constant ringing. When I didn't respond to this type of privacy invasion he started harassing my ex-husband, my adult children and my senior parents.

It took two years to gather enough evidence to arrest him, but the Rensselaer, New York District Attorney's Office was determined to help me. He was finally arrested and convicted of aggravated harassment.

There are twelve more months left of his 36-month probationary period and my hope is that he'll move on and leave me alone. Only time will tell.

Surviving any type of victimization is never easy and from the beginning I turned to friends and my family for support. One of them encouraged me to see a therapist who helped me regain my strength and self-confidence. But, it was the daily support from friends and family that helped me through the terror. As fear took over my life many of my friends slept over or went shopping for me when I was too frightened to leave the house.

Those who were handy with tools installed motion detectors, light timers, and new locks and helped in any way they could to make me feel safer. Others volunteered to take my calls of frustration, whenever I needed to talk, no matter what time of the day. My chain of friendship stretched to California and with the time zone differences I had a connection through 2AM EST.

Some volunteered to teach me self-defense or others, even though I did not do it, wanted to teach me to shoot a gun. If I needed financial support, other friends stood by with checkbook in hand. None of them judged me for staying in this relationship as long as I had. They only saw a friend hurting and afraid and they all stepped "up to the plate." I grew strong because of their support and encouragement and my own determination grew as we jointly vowed not to "Let this man win."

Struggling to overcome harassment and stalking I realized that our area did not have any type of formal support group and I became determined to start one.

I approached the Crime Victims Assistance Program of Troy, NY and regional victim assistance history was rewritten. The woman who served as organizer, co-leader and my advocate is now a dear friend. Together we have helped many women, giving them strategies and advice. As an advocate, my friend has accompanied women to court, worked with police and the district attorney's office.

1998, this friend organized speakers for Crime Victims Awareness Week and asked me to share my story. I did. I have also spoken at Take Back the Night rallies and I now serve on the Capital Region Anti Stalking Task Force.

Through my own resolve and the help of those who loved me I was able to turn a horrible situation into something positive for the community. When I faced the ex-boyfriend and read my victim's impact statement in court, the room was filled with over thirty of my friends, including my ex-husband and therapist. I cannot imagine how my journey would have ended without the support of those who love me but I do recognize that without them my journey would have been more frightening and lonely. It is a victory we all share, it is a testimony to friendship and what it can accomplish.

Marjorie Leibowitz

p.s. If you'd like more information you can visit our website at www.stalkmenot.org

Dear _____,

Several years ago, I walked out on my husband and three small children. I was an alcoholic and an up and coming drug addict. It was the hardest decision I thought I'd have to make in my life, but my reasoning was that they'd be better off, and safer without me around. The truth was I wanted to party and with so much in my way, I couldn't.

So, I took the coward's way out and left them. But, I realize that I needed some help and in a big way.

To say that I grew up in a dysfunctional family would be putting it mildly.

My father molested me, along with a couple of boys until I was eight years old. I felt unwanted and unloved by my mother. I cannot remember a time when she showed any affection to me, then when she died two weeks after my 11th birthday, talk about mad! After that we were shipped off to another state to live with people we didn't know, they were totally unprepared for three more kids.

Anyway, after ten years of hard partying, I got involved with a group of people that I should never have been with. They had money and exciting lives and I wanted a part of that. I got it and more, we ended up getting arrested and sent to prison. Talk about culture shock! Once I got out I tried to stay straight and become a good citizen but after 23 job refusals I threw in the towel and started drinking which led to other things.

I of course got busted on dirty urine and was given a choice of jail or a recovery program. I knew in my heart that I couldn't take anymore so I half-heartedly decided on the rehab not realizing that it was going to last a lifetime.

I fought tooth and nail but there was a counselor that finally reached deep and with her help I finally started to come to grips with my past and myself. She found that with music we could relate. Do you know the song Desperado by the Eagles? Well, I thought I was destined to be alone and unloved and to never have what I wanted in life. Then there was my probation officer, she was so with it, in charge and in control and I wanted to be like that. Of course I never told her that. She had so much faith in me and I know she wanted me to succeed. She was like a mother hen. You should have seen it when I brought my boyfriend to meet her! But, her approval was important to me and I tried so hard to win it.   To this day, almost 7 years later, I try to keep in touch with her.

Recovery is a blessing and so is my life now. My children talk to me and send me their babies' pictures.

I am remarried to a really nice man and I have a baby of my own. It's been almost ten years since I've had a drink or a drug and don't get me wrong it can still be tempting, but with the help of my family and a Higher Power it does get easier. Never give up hope, don't let anything keep you from living a good life.

There are so many good people willing to help you only need to ask.

Sincerely,

Found My Way.

Dear_____,

It all started 3 days after my 9th birthday. I was awaken by hands running up and down my body. I tried to jump out of my bed and couldn't because of the death grip on my arm. I tried to scream but he had his hand over my mouth. I had trouble breathing.

Who was this man and why was he hurting me like this? When it finally ended, which felt like forever, he left. I lay there crying and feeling so much pain I could hardly move.

This went on for about 3 years. Every night I lay in my bed trying not to fall asleep.

At the age of 10, I started using marijuana. I thought it would help me forget what was happening to me. By the time I was 12 I started drinking alcohol. The drugs seemed to help ease everything I was feeling. There wasn't a day that went by that I wasn't drunk or high. Not only was I being sexually abused, I was also becoming an addict.

I started failing school, losing my friends and worst of all, I was losing myself. I changed in so many ways, my attitude, my appearance. I just didn't care about anything or anyone. I was becoming a person I hated more than anyone else. The drugs and alcohol seemed to help me through this pain, or so I thought. At the age of 13, it happened again for the last time. I knew what he was doing wasn't right. He was not doing this to me because he loved me.

I went and confided in my school counselor. I knew my decision to tell my mother was the right thing to do. She had seen a change in me and thought it was a stage I was going through. She didn't want to believe what was going on. I remember her staring into my eyes and then she knew it was the truth. I remained in counseling for a few years. This is exactly what I needed. Not only did I learn how to deal with all the pain and different feelings that I had, it taught me to forgive this man, my brother.

I learned that even though he told me that what he did to me he did because he loved me and it was ok, he really did it because he had a sickness himself. He also went into therapy. I love my brother very much and I have forgiven him because we both got the help we needed. He recently died of cancer at the age of 42.

I'll never get over all the pain and feelings I have but I'm learning how to deal with them. I have a prayer that also helps me with life in general. It really does help me get through the day. "God grant me the serenity to accept the things I can not change, the courage to change the things I can and the wisdom to know the difference." I truly do live by this prayer. It has taught me to deal with each situation one day at a time.

From

Sexually Abused

Chapter Reflections

Introduction to Chapter 3

Dear _____,

You haven't been forgotten. Help is on the Way! I can't tell you the number of times that I've been through a difficulty in my life and just when I thought I would break, the answer came or the need was met. I hope that when you read the letters in this chapter you will realize that God is always there for you and will provide for you.

Read on and be encouraged!

Elaine

Galations 6-9

Let us not be weary in doing well, for in the proper time we will reap a harvest if we do not give up.

Help Is On The Way!

Dear _____,

I had been faking it! It seemed like I was just walking down the road unsure and sometimes uncaring where it was leading because I was just so tired of trying to do the very best I could yet not seeing my situation change. Have you ever felt like that? The harder you try the worst things seem to get and the end seems nowhere in sight.

That was me! No joy inside and the misery showed on the outside. I was just going through the motions.

I wanted to accomplish so many things in life, not just for myself, but to help others too. But, it was like I was at a standstill. And everything I did seemed mundane, boring, and aggravating.

Trying to get to the better job, the better career, and the better opportunities was just zapping all my strength and it was beginning to show.

Thank God that a very caring and observant friend noticed me. She walked up to me one day at work and said "I have something for you". If memory serves me correct, she said she'd had this "something" for a while and had been meaning to bring it to work, but had forgotten.

The next day, she brought it and simply said, "Here you go."

I love gifts, not so much surprises, but I love to get a gift. I also love to give gifts. But, that day I was on the receiving end. I took the gift, what I thought was a card and put it in my purse. When I got home, exhausted as usual, I reached into the purse remembering that I had a gift that I now hoped would cheer me up. I began to open the envelope and could see it was a card and as I continued to unwrap it I noticed there was a CD too. The card had a beautiful ladybug on the front of it and it was blank inside, except for the words that she had written:

Dear Diva:

I'm not really sure how to start this....

I just wanted to say that I know sometimes work gets you down and it makes you feel un-appreciated. So, I decided to give you a solution for the moments when life is getting you down. The first song is for you to know that you are the greatest no matter what! The second is to let you know that someone holds you with the highest regards. You are loved by many and I don't think you get to hear it often, so from my heart, good luck, no matter where life takes you and know that I appreciated our friendship and hold you dear to my heart.

Always,

Then, she signed her name.

When I finished reading the letter I put on the CD and it was a song by R. Kelly titled "The Greatest". As I listened to the lyrics, I began to cry. The song spoke about having your back against the ropes and that was exactly how I was feeling. The more the song played, the more I cried until I began to scream and then wail as I lamented, mourned for myself.

How could she know? How could she know that I felt so beaten up, or more specifically beaten down? My wailing turned into praise and I screamed "THANK YOU, THANK YOU GOD, SOMEBODY KNOWS, SOME-BODY KNOWS MY STRUGGLE".

I was still screaming when the next song started. It was a song by Celine Dion and R. Kelly, titled "I'm your angel". When I heard the lyrics, I started up again. I screamed and wailed and I did so the entire song. After the song had ended, I just sat there on the floor. I was crying softly now and talking to God. "My hope was gone and you sent someone to help. You know exactly what is happening to me. You know how painful it is to be where I am. You know how hard this is, I cried."

When I finally came to myself I was calm and I felt like a weight had literally been lifted off my shoulders. I also felt loved because I knew without a doubt that when I first began to get off center, that's when this "true friend" had noticed me. And, her heart had been touched to do something for me. It wasn't until sometime later that I got this "gift', but God had been thinking about me when I first started to hurt.

What a great gift! It's a gift I now pass on to you, Dear Weary. Fret not, God knows and those two songs are for you just as much as they are for me. You are the greatest because you have stayed in the race. You have made it this far, despite the odds.

You have to keep going, keep trying, keep pushing. Don't be weary in doing the right thing, the upright thing, stand, get off the ropes and in due season you shall reap a harvest. I know because not long (about a year) after I got her CD I began receiving my harvest. My attitude started to change, my health improved, and awards and numerous opportunities came my way.

Hallelujah!

Elaine Houston

Dear _____,

One day you are riding down life's road wondering how to squeeze your obligations of managing work and family into the hours remaining in the day. And, just as quickly, life can shift and change!

My father died in May and I was devastated by his death. I looked for ways to deal with the pain of the loss. I grieved for what was and what will never be! I turned to my mother for an answer to "How do I move forward'? I never acquired the answer from my mother because in July of that same year, she was diagnosed with cancer and I became a caretaker.

My world changed dramatically and I had to meet the challenges of caring for my mother whose role shifted from independence to dependence.

In the midst of despair appeared a woman, angel, who was sincere, giving, and whom unselfishly impacted our lives. I was so wrapped up and involved in my life that I was not conscious of the blessing. Sister Viola Jones, a dedicated and devoted member of my church and the community, came into my presence, offering the calmness of wisdom. She listened, advised, prayed, loved and encouraged me. Sister Jones amplified objectivity. She helped me to reach beyond myself and understand that the woman before me, my mother, was fighting her own battle. She too, was dealing with her loss, the loss of my father and her independence. The hurtful words my mother uttered were a part of her own torment.

I observed in silence as Sister Jones read from the Bible to my mother, prayed and sang to my mother.

Some of my most unforgettable moments came one day when my mother joined in and sang her favorite song with Sister Jones, or the day my mother was so weak, but found just enough strength to repeat "AMEN" after Sister Jones said a prayer.

Sister Jones supported me through each step and fallback of my healing.

Somewhere along the way, I forgot that situations and people are beyond our control and that we can only change ourselves. I am so grateful that she touched and enriched my life. The abilities to cope and endure are empowerments that I will continually share with others.   We control our lives! We have the choice of living and re-shaping our life or handing over our biography and allowing others to control our destiny.

Sister Jones' support helped to restore my fading strength, the strength needed to continue and finish the tasks before me.   She is truly a blessing! Blessings come in many forms. We must only open the door!

Luvenia Cleveland

Dear _____,

I'm writing this letter to you to testify to the goodness of my Lord and Savior, Jesus Christ, who supplies all my needs according to his riches in glory.

A few years ago, during the beginning of my walk with the Lord, I had just had major surgery and had been out of work for about 4 weeks. There was no money coming in because the disability payments were backed up. My son was going on a field trip with his school and needed money for lunch. I had no way of getting any money, or so I thought. But, my God touched the hearts of a husband and wife in the congregation and they came to me separately and privately, without a big fuss and they allowed God to use them to bless me as well as my son.

I know that God is a good God and he can do anything but fail. Please be encouraged and know that whatever you're going through, God is able to work it out. Just open your heart and receive him.

Sister Diane Nobles

p.s. God has since provided me with a blessed and saved husband.

Dear _____,

There are times during my life when I wish someone had told me everything would turn out okay, that troubled times eventually fade away.

When life throws us a curve ball, we do have the ability to survive and pick ourselves up.

Situations in life can seem dire. It may feel as if our life is over and that times will never get better. But, what doesn't kill us DOES make us stronger.

Life has thrown me a few curve balls. One was growing up with an alcoholic father.

My father would yell and scream so loud the neighbors would hear. I remember seeing my mother cry. And, I don't think there's anything more upsetting than seeing your mother hurting. Plus, there was nothing I could do to help her. I felt helpless. I felt as if no one cared and that there was no way out of the situation. I would cry myself to sleep because I didn't know what to do.

Dramatic and desperate thoughts went through my head. Thoughts too crazy, I would probably be arrested if I shared them now. I hated my father. I hated my life. It was at these low points I wish I knew that life would get better. I wish I knew that there was going to be a happy ending. Knowing this would have helped me not lose faith, because I did lose faith. I lost faith in God and in myself. I lost faith in life itself.

But then a miracle did happy. Despite my betrayal to spiritual confidence, life got better. My father sought help and became sober. It was as if he was a new person. My family's lives changed profoundly. We shared our feelings with each other. We expressed our anger. Things got pretty rocky, but most importantly we were talking and communicating. A relationship I never thought possible with my father was born. And, finally I felt good about life.

Dear sisters, I wish I had known that life would turn out okay. I wish I had known that life could get better, no matter how low it seemed. Rainbows do appear after a rainstorm. I think if I had known this, I wouldn't have lost faith in myself. Times can seem bleak. It may feel as if the world is ending, but don't give up faith. Miracles can happen.

Sincerely,

A Survivor

Dear_____,

At one point in my life I used to carry the last name of "Ms. Timid"
Today, I'm now referred to as "Ms. Determination."

For years I was thought of as being weak and too sensitive. I heard it
so much that I actually started believing it.

Oh! How I tried to change, just to be able to be accepted by the one
who I thought loved me. Little did I know that I had to love myself—
First!
Once I came to the place of self-love, I found out that I had courage.
I also had the determination to stand up and declare, "I am fearfully
and wonderfully made."

So if you are known as "Ms. Timid look inside yourself and begin to
love the person you truly are. You will eventually find out your real
name, the new name God had intended for you all along.

Azalea Smith

Dear _____,

I hope that this letter finds its way to you somehow. If I could address it to someone I would address it to "Dear Wishful."

As you read these words, please know that they are written with love and a sincere wish for your health, happiness and your well being.

Hear me out, for our time is short and the space here brief, but my message wields great power to change your life for the better, if you let it. Who am I, you ask? I'm simply someone who has been there. See, I was "you" not long ago and more than once or thrice. I've done my share of wishful thinking, always ending up with nothing more than empty wishes that left you down and out, unsure of yourself, and unhappy in life.

Take growing up. It was hard for me. I wanted so badly to have blond hair and blue eyes. I wanted to look like all the other kids. I wanted to have what everyone else had. I wanted to be just like them in every way.

But the truth is, I simply didn't look like them, didn't have what they had and couldn't be just like them if I tried, no matter how much I may have wished it.

Even in adulthood, there have been not-too-distant times when I've wished in vain, loved and lost, sought but never found. And, each time, I would lament the losses and cry silently to myself over the "could-have-beens." I remember wondering why me. I remember wishing that I could be almost anyone but who I really am.

But, I've learned a thing or two since then, and so too, will you. As you journey through life, its important to not get caught up in the disappointments or dwell on that which wasn't meant to be. Wishes are good, but never lose sight of what is real in your life. Rather, treasure every joy, every sorrow, every laugh, and every tear. Yes, and even every heartbreak, for it's the rainy days that help us appreciate the sun.

Now, and then, I wish I could have back all the time that I wished away, the youth and the years that have passed and the moments I've wasted along the way. But I wish only in passing now, because the truth is I've learned to live in the present, to celebrate the good without forgetting to learn from the bad. I recognize now that the lessons of life are invaluable in whatever shape they take because they ultimately shape who we are.

So, I offer you this page from my book and the lessons I've learned. You see, wishing and wanting for things, or people, or situations do not make them so. Life, fulfillment and happiness are what we make them, and what must come to us from within ourselves.

Realize life is a privilege and our time on earth is all too brief. Do not forsake it. Live each day and each moment to the fullest. Appreciate the people and all that you have in your life. Don't wait to tell someone that you love them. Believe in someone special and always believe in yourself. And, don't be afraid to care, love, wish and dream too.

Keep these words close to your heart and they'll help you long after these pages are yellow with age. And though there may be difficult times ahead or obstacles along the way, hold strong and steady in your belief that everything happens for a reason. That is my wish for you. Endure, trust, have faith and one day, you'll understand as I do. Til then, I wish you well.

With love,

Angela

Dear_____,

You are on the verge of a miracle. The question is how bad do you want it?

Did God say you could have it? What must you do to attain it?

In November 1997 I was forced to leave my home because the government decided to buy the home I had rented for thirteen years. I know God had whispered in my ear that He wanted me to prepare to own my own home. Stop spending, reduce debt, start a savings account, pay off some things. I must be honest. I had very little faith then. I have great faith now.

God had to force me out of my comfort zone in order to ignite my faith. He's probably doing the same thing to you.

I looked for a house under my own power. I thought I had consulted God, but what I was really doing was finding a house and asking Him to bless my choice. Wrong move. In April of 2000 during (Cleansing Streams), a class taught at my church which guides you through steps on how to leave all your baggage and troubles at the alter, I acknowledged I had not consecrated my son Robert Alexander, my daughter Kirstin Annette, my life or my search for a home to the Lord. I repented. That was on a Tuesday.

The very next day my current neighbor, a godly woman I've known for twenty years, told me about the house next to her going on the market. I called the realtor and saw the house. God said yes in my spirit. That's when the warfare began. For one week the realtor would not return my calls. Finally, I was able to talk to him. He said the bank wanted "cash" at closing. This was not the truth. The devil wanted me to give up but I heard the voice of the Lord say "How bad do you want it? " I said "I will fast until I hear yes." The devil instantly said "You're going to die.' I reached up and pulled down pit bull faith.

God put me on a total fast, which started on Wednesday. I asked God to instruct me and direct me. He spoke as clear as I'm writing to you. Each step I took did not always get an instant reaction. I stayed on course. The house was in foreclosure. God gave me the name of the bank and put me in touch with the person who was responsible for my house. On Saturday my realtor wrote the offer. The following Monday, I was released from the fast when I heard yes. The bank accepted my offer of 29,000 dollars. I closed on my house in May 2000.

I have a three bedroom home in one of the nicest neighborhoods in Rochester, New York. I have a nice yard with a tree that yields raspberries in the summer. I have a deck and during the remodeling process, I put a Jacuzzi in my home. My bedroom is the width of the house. I have hardwood floors upstairs. God did it !!!! The other two homes that I put an offer on were nowhere near as nice and sold for at least double the purchase price of my home.

I now know why God gave me this blessing. My children now have an inheritance from me when God calls me home to be with Him. Also, the blessing of the house is that it is truly a place of healing and ministering. Those who are hurting come here to be refreshed and healed. There is tremendous peace in every room throughout the house. God's presence definitely dwells on the very property He has given me. I offer my home as a place of refuge and rest. It's really a gift from God, which I give back to Him on a daily basis.

Whatever God has promised you. He is faithful to bless you with the ability to obtain and possess that which you stand firm in faith in until you have received the promise. Don't back up, don't stand still, don't give up, don't give in, don't rely on yourself. Trust God and stand, believing God is with you.

Cheryl A. Scott

Dear_____,

We all need to be reminded at times; reminded of how strong we are as women, reminded that as women we do have power, reminded that we are winners. What do you need to be reminded of?

One of my most important reminders came from my friend Carolyn. She reminded me to not give up and to dream again.

I have always been a dreamer. As a young child, I fantasized stories in my mind. I created them in my head from beginning to end and they always had a happy ending. I could just sit and imagine things. Imagine the plot, the protagonist, the antagonist, I came up with all the dialogue, all in my head, it was all in my mind.

As a young adult, just out of college I dreamed too. I dreamt of being a foreign correspondent, telling the stories of others from all over the world. After college, I pounded the pavement, looking for a job with a bright smile and a degree in Journalism.
It took me seven years to find that first job.

Once, I finally made it into the business, I realized that telling the stories of others would not be quite the job I had envisioned in my dreams. I had the zeal, the zest for the business, the dogged determination, but I had never been prepared for the politics of the business.

At one television station in particular, I was treated very badly. I was over looked and left out of assignments. I was not the favorite and I think it had to do with me asserting myself. In fact, whenever I stood up for myself, there were repercussions. My boss wouldn't even acknowledge me, wouldn't even speak to me, for months. He would turn his head in the opposite direction when I approached him or when we met by accident in the hall. He was a very arrogant man and was very haughty and heavy handed whenever he had to deal with me. He was a man whom my colleagues would dismiss by saying, 'He's just not a people person." They too knew that he should not have been in the position of managing people.

It was a terrible working environment. I was miserable! I did everything in my power to try and find another job and leave.

Carolyn knew about what was happening to me and loved and supported me through the many trials I faced on that job.

She often sent me encouraging cards, or called me and left uplifting messages. One day she sent me an e-mail that as soon as I read it got me back on track. Here's what it said:

Dear Elaine,

You are not just another pretty face but a vessel of God that is destined to continue being a conduit for his blessings to others. He will not forsake one who does so much for his name's sake. I pray for you daily. God bless you, your friend Carolyn.

Just below the email was a picture of a young African girl with just the sweetest smile. She was adorned in her native clothing and wore cultural jewelry. Her hands were clasped and she looked the picture of serenity but there was also what appeared to be a spear or large knife at her side. Under her picture there was a story about a brave young African warrior princess named Nzinga Mbande. She inherited the throne of Mbande in 1624 and waged war on her enemies and led her people to independence.

Young Nzinga may have looked sweet but she also knew how to fight. I knew how to fight too, how to persevere in spite of the challenges and Carolyn's e-mail reminded me of that.

Not too long after I read about young Nzinga, I started dreaming again. I dreamt of telling stories again, stories about people from all around the world and I realized I needed to do it right where I was, in my prison. I couldn't wait until my boss started to respect me and appreciate me. So, I totally removed thoughts of us ever getting along from my mind. I learned to seek appreciation from the people who loved me and knew me. We all want to be appreciated and there's nothing wrong with that. But, it comes from your friends, like Carolyn and your family. I had to stop looking for appreciation in this hostile environment. I had to stop taking the way my boss responded to me personally. And, I began to learn that some times no matter how hard you try there will be people that you will never get along with.

There's a verse in the Bible that talks about being at peace with others and treating all people kindly, but it also acknowledges that you may "not" be able to be at peace with everyone.

So, I made my peace with my boss, inside myself. I concentrated on the dream I had. I came up with a new feature where I tried to bring to the viewers stories on people who were using their lives to make the lives of others better. I loved it! I believe the reason these stories satisfied me so is because I tried so hard to have that kind of life for myself. Everybody has a story to tell. Everybody is important. And, I want to use my life to tell their stories. I want to do stories that improve, encourage and help others appreciate their lives and make the most of it. This book is an extension of that dream.

In this book there are stories about women from all across the world, from Jamaica, Rwanda, Congo, Middle East, and throughout the United States.

Before Carolyn's email, I thought I'd never get to be that foreign correspondent because I was at the mercy of my boss who couldn't see my potential, and office politics.

Once I realized I was really in control of my own future I started looking for stories outside the norm, stories that were foreign to others. Even though it did not happen the way I had hoped it would, I really became that foreign correspondent.

If you have forgotten how to dream because you're struggling right now, in the middle of a nightmare, try creating your own way by taking the road no one has gone down. Set yourself apart, instead of trying to be a part of the group. The chances are excellent that you will fulfill your dreams, but in a way more beautiful and more spectacular than you ever imagined. You will live the life God meant for you, instead of the life you planned for yourself.

Elaine Houston

Dear _____,

"Hello." "Hi Gina, it's me Trisha." "Hi Trisha, how are you?" "Good." 'How are you doing?" "I'm good too." "Momma said you moved into your own apartment." "Yea! I did. I like it a lot. It's small but it's nothing like having your own." "Did daddy tell you about me?" "Yea, he did." "The doctor said I'm HIV positive."

I got a phone call from one of my sisters that changed my life. Although I had known before she called me, she called to tell me herself that she was infected with the HIV virus. I knew the life my sister lived, at least in part. Other family members always knew more than I did because they were closer to her and I lived so far away. God gives us wisdom and he tells us in the Bible that you reap what you sow. Understanding this I still ignored the fact that my sister could ever get sick. We were" born" in the church. Our parents were Christians. For heavens' sake my dad was a minister. This could not happen to my sister and to my family.

It had happened and my job now was to pray. Earnestly I had to pray to God for him to please heal my sister. This can be a miracle not often seen and my sister would live and not die. I could see my sister praising God in church, dancing for joy for her healing.

Over the course of about two years, things got worse for my sister and this led my family and I to pray more. I really believed God would heal her so that everyone could see that she was not sick anymore.

I had never been so alone in my life. I was the farthest from home and could do the least for her. Please heal her God. Please heal her. She'll have a testimony to tell the world. She'll give her life to you and she'll stay with you. No more backsliding. She'll stay this time. At times I begged God to take this sickness away and let my sister please live.

Trisha was happy for me having my own apartment. She said she was proud of her baby sister.

Two years after I got my own apartment, I got another phone call, but not from Trish. This call was to tell me that my sister had passed away. What an empty feeling I had. Talk about a hole in your heart. It was so unexplainable but it was so, so real.

God blessed a woman to come fellowship at my church and she would often testify of the love of Christ. She gave her testimony of sickness and of healing from the HIV virus.

She so blessed me in her testimony because I could see my sister in her. God didn't do it for my blood relative but He did do it. So many things I prayed to God for, for my sister were coming forth in this lady's testimony and praise to God.

I thank God today because through a testimony of witness of God's great love and power, God blessed me to see that He did answer my prayer. Maybe not with Trisha, although now I know she is healed, but with another sister, a sister in Christ.

Through someone else He answered me.

Gina

Chapter Reflections

Introduction to Chapter 4

Dear _____,

Hey there WOMAN, I hear you roaring like a mighty lioness. And, what you're saying is that you have climbed the corporate ladder, crashed through the glass ceiling, changed the status quo, chartered some new courses and turned the word NO into the word ON, as in, BRING IT ON.

 You've have brought about unity where there was none. You have led an army where there was no sergeant. You overcame the word "Overcome" and when asked how you did it you simply said, "IT'S A WOMAN THING'

Elaine

Proverbs 1-20

Wisdom calls aloud in the street, she raises her voice in the public squares.

It's A Woman Thing!

Dear  _____,

Most of my major accomplishments started out with me wondering whether I could really do the task at hand. In fact, one of my most vivid successes started out that way. It was January 2000. I was a television reporter working in Albany, NY.

A couple of years earlier, I had done a story on a Cuban-American businessman who was seeking public office. It was a relevant story because while there was a very noticeable Hispanic population, there were no local Latinos in public office. This gentleman was going for even bigger fish by trying to unseat our well-known U.S. Congressman, who came from a well known, local, political family. I found the story intriguing because I love stories about the underdog.

The businessman did not win but he liked my story. So, now that he was planning a humanitarian trip to his native land, he remembered me and wanted me to go along and report on what his fact-finding commission had found.

I attempted to sell the story to my executive producer who in turn attempted to sell it to my News Director.   The answer that came back was no!   I was told it was too expensive of a trip.

But, I persisted. To cut the cost, I suggested that the station's only female photographer go with me. We could share a room and save money.   I got no response. I persisted but only in my mind.

I knew this was a great opportunity and even before this chance came my way I had been petitioning God to give me a big story, a great opportunity.

You see, although I had been at the station for 11 years, I had only gotten two out of town assignments. I knew I could cover the bigger stories but the trick was to get one!

So, when this chance came up, even though I had been turned down, I clearly remember hearing God say "Don't get angry" so in my spirit, there was a calmness.

I had asked God for a chance and I knew he would give it to me. Then, something happened!

It was almost Thanksgiving and a little Cuban boy had been discovered on a raft near the coast of Miami. His mother and others had died. His name was Elian Gonzalez. Already a controversy was brewing, should the little boy remain in Miami with relatives or be sent back home to Cuba to his father.   I immediately, went back to my EP. I reminded her that I would be the only local television reporter and what a great exclusive this would be. The answer came back YES!

Then, a week before I was suppose to go, I got sick with a wicked cold and wondered if I would be able to go. I made up in my mind I would go sick or not.

People always ask me if I'm nervous before I go on the air or do a live report and I explain to them that it's more of an adrenalin rush than nervousness. But, I have to admit I had some moments of fear about this trip, mainly because some in the group were fearful. There was talk of our rooms being bugged and cameras catching our every move. The controversy surrounding the little Cuban boy also fueled my apprehension.

But, my fears soon subsided, when I got to Cuba and met the people. They were engaging, proud and warm. Even though they were poor, they were educated and had dreams and there was such a respect for the family unit. I ended up doing six stories, including the discovery of the childhood home of a local doctor in the group who was returning to Cuba after 30 years or so.

His family fled Cuba when Castro came to power, leaving everything. The family who now lived in the house was still using his family's appliances. His family's crest, like the rings around an old tree, was still visible in some of the furniture and told a story about both families. And, what an unbelievable story it was!

I accomplished so many things in Cuba. And, I never in my life felt as capable, credible and blessed as I did covering this trip. When you cover a story out of town, you work 16 hour days. You do the work of a producer and reporter. When you're out of the country its even worse, you have to constantly think on your feet, conceptualize every story and know the exact shots and get all the interviews you need because once you leave there's no chance of going back to shoot more.

This trip brought out abilities that had been dormant, unused, things I did not know I possessed. It forced me to respond and stand up to situations many people would have given up on. It made me move beyond the point of impossibilities until I accomplished what I came for. It was frustrating and exhilarating at the same time and proved to me that given the chance I could handle any story.

I will remember many of the experiences I had in Cuba but one that has left an indelible mark on me is a rally I attended for the little Cuban boy, Elian Gonzales. Although, I was in the country to cover the humanitarian delegation, I found out that there was going to be a march by angry mothers, upset that the U-S was not returning Elian. I was told thousands would be rallying for this little boy. Knowing this was a huge story, I broke with the delegation and found an interpreter and was set to attend the rally the following morning. Unlike my other stories this was breaking news and I had to get this story back to Albany in time for the 5pm news.

However, I ran into a snag when my interpreter decided to ditch me at the last minute and work with a network reporter, presumably for more money. My "Espanol" was ok for giving directions but I didn't feel capable of being on my own heading to a site in a foreign country. But, after I lost my translator I was indeed on my own.

So, the next morning, my photographer and I got a cab and told the driver to take us to the site of the rally. The driver refused, saying he could only take me within blocks of the event. He was obviously afraid of something and when we got out of the cab I understood what it was. The site of the rally was surrounded by a show of unimaginable force. Armed police were everywhere, lining the streets for blocks. They were standing shoulder to shoulder and looked very impressive and very threatening.

When we got out of the cab, we were immediately swept up into this great throng of people. They were all walking to the site and you really had to watch your step or you would literally run over someone.

It was an incredible sight and feeling and just like everyone else we followed the crowd. I knew that I needed to get interviews before the march began, but again I was worried about my Spanish.

As I scanned the crowds I noticed a gaggle of video photographers, still photographers and foreign press. So, we walked up, introduced ourselves and found a still photographer from New York. He also spoke Spanish. I asked him to help me out and he translated my questions to the people I interviewed. Just as we finished the march began.

It was a march consisting of all women. (It was called the Mother's March) Some were pushing strollers, others were walking hand in hand with their children. Leading the crowd was Elian's family, his step-mother, infant stepbrother and his grandmother. The crowd was at least 30 across but the length was innumerable. Estimates were that 10,000 people had turned out. As I watched row after row pass in front of me I wondered if there was anything in the U-S that would bring people out like that. What could unite us?

I later saw rows and rows of buses lined up at the end of the route and I realized that the people had been bussed in. Were they forced to take part? Or, were they bussed in because they have no transportation? I was skeptical, but I was also in a communist country.

We finished shooting and began to head back to the hotel but I took a moment to breath it all in. Here I was a child who grew up in a single parent household, a child who lived in a housing project, the first in my family to finish college and now I was standing in a communist country reporting on a story that was making headlines around the world, signing off, Elaine Houston, Newschannel 13, Havana, Cuba.

I could have cried crocodile tears right there! I asked my photographer to take a picture of me. (I still look at it when I need inspiration)

We headed back to the hotel where I finished writing the story and recorded my script onto a tape in the camera. It was still very early but I wanted to get this story back to the U-S as soon as possible. I was feeling good that I had overcome the translator issue and had gotten the interviews and had written the story, little did I know the hard part was just beginning.

We headed downstairs and hailed a cab to take us to Cuban television where we would feed back the story.

We arrived at the television station and after waiting for about a half hour were told to go down the street to another building, which we recognized as the place we got our press credentials. While there, we ran into our translator who ditched us! She was surprised to see us and we her, because her excuse for ditching us was that she was sick. Feeling that I was not where I needed to be I went walking the halls talking to people trying to make sure we were in the right place. I met a guy who told me I needed to go back down the street to the building I'd just come from. We did and after repeated attempts to get them to understand I was from NBC and needed to send a tape they let us go to the control room.

In Cuba if you learn nothing else you learn that long lines and waiting was inevitable but I wasn't having it that day! My gut was telling me to speak up and be assertive and after waiting for 20 minutes with no one coming to my rescue, I told my photographer to stay put and I started walking the halls again, looking for help. I had tenacity, I had charm and I was persistence. But, none of those traits seemed to be enough. Finding a seat I sat and started to pray. "God, I know you did not send me this far for me to not get my story on the air. Tell me what to do, I prayed."

"Thank you, I said", and I got up and walked down the hall looking for someone. That's when I ran into a Cuban reporter. She spoke the same amount of English as I did Spanish. We went back and got my photographer and then went upstairs to a room that looked like a nerve center. We explained my plight to one of the engineers and I knew there was a God because he spoke English and told me that I would have to have the station's name on a tape feed list.

Where was I from, he wanted to know. Forget Albany, New York..."I said I'm from NBC, New York. His eyes lit up, "NBC" yes, he said with a toothy smile. To get on the list my station would have to set up the coordinates. So, I asked for a phone he showed me one and I called Albany. And, the craziness began again, but this time on my end. I WAS PUT ON HOLD! SOMEONE IN MY NEWSROOM PUT ME ON HOLD. Then, I was disconnected!!!!!

But, I had no time to get mad. I called back. IT HAPPENED AGAIN! I called back, this time I called the operator and yelled, I'm in Cuba don't put me on hold.   She transferred me to the newsroom and in about another hour, I saw the station's name on the Cuban "TAPE FEED" list.   I cheered and the Cuban engineer laughed.

Now, it was time to head back down stairs and send the story, which still needed to be edited in Albany. I had missed the 5:00 news and the 5:30, but finally, over the phone, which I refused to hang up, I heard my voice on the tape, back in Albany. I thanked the person in Albany, receiving the tape and hung up.   I thanked the Cuban engineer and I thanked God.   My photographer and I headed out of the building and into the cool Cuban air. I looked at her, raised my hand to "HI FIVE" her and walked with confidence back to the hotel. All I could think of was "YOU GO GIRL"!!!!!!

Elaine Houston

Dear _____,

In May 1999, three of my colleagues from Niagara Mohawk Power Company and I headed to Washington, DC to attend a national utilities conference for Consumer Advocates. Consumer Advocates assist low-income customers in accessing financial assistance from government.

I took the train from Albany, NY and on the train, I happened to sit with three women from a local non-profit agency. They too were bound for DC but for a national convention of social workers. We all made plans to meet for dinner on the last night of both conferences.

On the night of the dinner, I brought along two of my female col-leagues from Niagara Mohawk. One woman from the social workers convention also joined us. Steve, the lone male advocate, opted to call it a night, after the conference.

After dinner, we headed for the Metro, it was just a short ride. It was a beautiful evening in May. We got off at the National Portrait Gallery and proceeded to walk the one lady the short distance to her hotel, before heading on to ours.

I don't know when it occurred to me to look around, but when I did, I noticed the barred storefronts, lots of graffiti, and broken streetlights. I also noticed a guy about two blocks away. But, because there were four of us, I felt we were ok. Plus, the hotel marquee blazed before us, within two blocks.

Was I wrong! Suddenly, that lone male, who had looked to be so far away, pushed between my friend and me, grabbed her purse and took off.

JoAnn had everything she owned in her purse. Also, I had encouraged her to come to the conference in the first place, her parents were both deceased and she had no one to call.

So, the four of us devised a plan. Three would chase, and the one who had cerebral palsy would remain on the corner under the one streetlight that was working, waiting for us to return.

The three of us ran, screaming through the night, after the mugger, running over deserted streets (we thought they were deserted; they weren't).

All of a sudden, three women we did not know joined us. They were sinewy and strong and they could run!

Then, two men who heard us ran up to us. One was a marathon runner, who had just completed his first marathon a week earlier. The other man repossessed cars. He asked which way the mugger had gone, and ran off in full pursuit.

Soon a Metropolitan police car pulled us over, asked questions, and then took off in pursuit too.

So the three of us, one with a scraped knee and another with a sore throat, hoarse from screaming decided to trudge back to the corner to meet our friend. She was still there, but was now surrounded by at least thirty women. They were the women from the social worker's conference. They had taken the same subway train and had followed the mugger. (We later found out that three from this group had run with us after the mugger). These women stayed with our friend, comforting her and then, when we returned, they took us under their wings and comforted us.

We all walked the last few blocks to the hotel, as sisters UNITED! As we walked, some of us were talked quietly, while others were angry. Some of us even started singing. But, not one of us felt despair, or hopelessness. How could we? We helped each other. What we also found out was the marathon runner had been coming from a dinner with his wife. She had now joined us and was walking back to the hotel, where she later met her husband.

At the hotel, at least fifty women joined our group, sitting around, having coffee and wine, just sharing stories. My two friends and I left hours later, after having shared one of the best nights of our lives!

The mugger was arrested, convicted and incarcerated. The police were quite surprised to see how we women banded together to help each other.

Just recounting the details gives me a wonderful sense of how we women, from all different backgrounds, banded together for one cause. This night was truly one of the best nights of my life.

p.s. And, you can be sure I think of what could have been and fortunately, wasn't.

Sue Nealon

Dear_____,

I was put here on this earth to lift and empower people through my voice. I was put here to lift up God and to magnify his name.   To lift his people to become empowered to move into their destiny. I love singing for God. It's a precious gift, to be anointed to serve him through song.

When you are in the midst of being used by God there is no other feeling like it on earth.
You are a vessel that he shines through at that moment to reach others. You enter into another realm of existence as he endows you with his anointing to impact lives for him. There is completeness like no other that takes place within.

Recording my first CD was an exciting experience. It took persistence and a lot of hard work. If you desire it, then GO FOR IT! But, know this:

Know the message that you are to give. Know your own heartbeat. Know what makes you sing from the inside out and remember to use your talent to serve God by using it to serve others.

Barbara Howard

Dear _____,

Sometimes as women we over analyze things. We actually go as far as becoming fearful of trying things. We give a verdict of failure even before reviewing all the evidence.

My desire was always to be able to stay home with my children. I wanted to do this to give my children a solid foundation of love and also a head start in their education.

But, when you look at life today and what it takes to raise a family I really saw no way of doing what I wanted. You are lead to believe that a family can't make it without dual incomes. I soon learned that with God all things are possible. I began to think of ways I could come home and still contribute to my household income.

Since I had a love for children it was suggested that I look into opening a home daycare. When I started my research on how to start this business I found out that there was so many resources available to me and I began to see that this venture was not as hard as I imagined. I started my business and not only did it succeed but God blessed in ways I would never have imagined. I formed relationships that are very important to me and still thrive today.

So, to you who have doubts about starting your own business I say trust God. I am a testimony of what God can and will do.

Azalea Smith

Dear_____,

What is your greatest accomplishment? As a woman, what would you say you've been able to achieve? When those questions were first asked of me my first response was to shrug my shoulders and so "Not Much". You see, I hadn't thought too long or hard about those questions.

But, wait a minute! These are soul searching questions and now that I've really thought about it, I can say. I AM A WOMAN OF WISDOM. I am also a survivor with unlimited potential. Those are my accomplishments!

For many years, issues and things had a stronghold on me. There were strong holds like anger about my father's incestuous behavior, feelings of inadequacy and the inability to express myself in words. There was also loneliness that started in childhood and remained with me throughout adulthood. I am surely a survivor. Gone are the echoes of that negative childhood criticism .No longer do I choose male relationships that stunt my growth and cause me to be forget how to be real with myself and to be positive.

For years my life was about pretending. I was so use to denying anger, pretending as a child and on into adulthood that things were o.k. All this pretending caused me to be physically and mentally sick.

However, when I learned the wisdom of forgiveness I was healed.

Now, instead of muteness, I am a woman who has learned to speak with courage. Instead of feelings of inadequacy, I know that I am sufficient. And I'm no longer lonely because I belong to a large and powerful family—the family of God.

Rhonda Green

Dear _____,

One of the greatest accomplishments of my life is still playing itself out.

And that accomplishment is the rebuilding of "me" after being torn down.

I never expected to be a mother- and to be a divorced mother with a son- well I certainly didn't expect that. After my first marriage crashed and burned, family members had some pretty interesting "Guestimations" about my value and whether or not I was redeemable.

They said I was "damaged goods" and I shouldn't hope that anyone would be interested in me. Talk about rebuilding from the ground up. First, I had to make it up off the ground. But, you know there is something special about a woman who says, "Lord, I don't know how to do this, I need your help." There is something special about women that we are not hindered in making this kind of admission. It changed my life and yes, I do believe that it is a woman thing.

After all the effort, time, talent, tears, discipline, budgeting, shopping, cleaning, cooking, washing, helping, correcting, monitoring, reading out loud and laughing it took, I am proud and grateful of how far I have come. No longer am I that scared, battered, little 20-something that I was.

I look in the mirror and I see waves and the shimmer of silver that are coming in and I see such beauty and achievement. There was a time when I couldn't picture myself being at this stage at all. It was all so desperate, so hand to mouth. It sure felt that way.

"When I look back over my life and think things over...are the lyrics to a gospel song that appropriately describes my achievements and my experiences thanks to the love, guidance and protection of my heavenly Father.

I've remarried since those scary days to someone who is kind, gentle, strong, funny and loving. God sent him to the "damaged goods" as one of his gifts of redemption. Who would have thought? My son is now 17, a senior in high school, preparing to go on with his life. Who would have thought?

When I talk about it being a woman thing... I mean just that. We women are special in God's sight and he comes to the rescue of a genuine heart, no matter what you've been called, no matter what's been done to you, no matter what you yourself have done.

Yeah, there have been accomplishments, achievements and I've reached goals and the best He says is yet to come. I am a mighty, strong, powerful and wise woman today because I dared to believe. Uh huh, sounds like a woman thing to me!

Kara Ford

Chapter Reflections

Introduction to Chapter 5

Dear _____,

This chapter is very, very special to me.

Had it not been for the person written about in this chapter, there would not be a book. Her name is Msevumba.

I first saw her in a series on "Nightline" about the people of the Democratic Republic of Congo. The country was destroyed by civil war and the women were the ones not only holding things together but, they were suffering as a result of being tortured and raped.

The series was called "Heart of Darkness". The night I saw Msevumba's story, it left me in tears. In this chapter, you'll read letters of encouragement from other women to the women in the Democratic Republic of Congo. They are really letters written to all women who are struggling against the odds, yet show remarkable strength through it all. Simply stated, these letters say, "We see you, we love you, we want to help you."

Elaine

Proverbs 31-15

She gets up while it is dark; she provides food for her family.

Letters To Msevumba

Dear Msevumba,

How are you? I pray that your family is well, your body is healthy and your spirit remains unbroken. I know that we have never met. In fact, we live in different villages, different countries, on different continents, but we have so much in common.

We share a history, a past and a future, because we are women. We are friends. You are my friend and I am now introducing you to my community, my state, my country, The World! You see, they "need" to meet you.

They need to know that you are a woman of virtue. Your work ethic inspires me, your love for your children and protection of them make me cry with hope.

It is because of you that I am a better person, a better woman— a much better friend. There is something between us Msevumba, a connection in our spirits, this thing, this sisterhood. It makes us no longer strangers, no longer distant, no longer different. We are the same. We want what is best for our children and our families. We have each seen suffering, tasted pain, and desired PEACE.

When you were crying inside, I saw you. I heard you! I understood. And, now I have come to help you. I'm bringing with me my friends, now your friends because we want to meet the woman who gets up while it is still dark; she provides for her family. That woman is blessed.

Sincerely,

Elaine Houston

Dear Msevumba,

I am honored to take part in this book to say a few words to you. First of all, I wish to tell you that I admire your strength, your courage, and your hard work. You are working hard to fulfill your commitment to your family. Your children's needs require this extraordinary strength to be met. Their lives are in your hands, just as yours was in your mother's. You have seen her strength and appreciated her hard work and she expects you to win the battle of raising your family.

Unfortunately, no matter how hard we try, there are still barriers that prevent us from improving the quality of our lives.

Endless wars and poverty pose a major challenge to African women, especially in the rural areas where infrastructures are almost inexistent. Your long miles walk under a skin burning sun to get to the nearest source of water, is a sign of how poverty affects the African woman's everyday life. Your everyday adventure in dangerous bushes to collect firewood, the youngest baby tied on your back and sometimes with another one due in a few months too, is beyond our understanding. In the midst of all your tough life your image, your sweat drops, captured many eyes and touched many hearts of women around the globe. Your bravery is amazing.

Someday, you will be rewarded for your hard work and it has already started because someone thought she would like to make a difference in your life, just like a woman named Wendy did in my case.

I hear your pain because I share some of your experiences. I used to walk miles to get water that was not even safe to drink. I collected firewood too, and I remember how hard it becomes during the tropical rain season. I remember the suffocating smoke that painted our kitchen black from its original gray sand coat. When the wet firewood wouldn't catch fire, my mother used paraffin to keep it burning. We were lucky enough to afford the paraffin cost. I wonder how you deal with the eyes-burning smoke.

Even though I may never meet you, I feel so close to you and will certainly keep thinking about you whenever I feel weak. Keep your African woman spirit high. We only survive because we believe in our strength and risk our own lives to save the lives of our children.

God bless you and your family.

Eugenie Mukeshimana

Dear Msevumba,

Greetings, in the name of the Lord Jesus Christ. God said fret not thyself because of evil doers neither be thou envious against the workers of iniquity because they shall soon be cut down like the grass and wither as the green herb. Msevumba I went back to God at the age of 30. I was attacked, forcibly raped and yes I had an encounter with incest also.

I didn't tell anyone. I took everything to God in prayer and He took the other party away. From then on I stayed close to my family and I stayed in prayer all the time. I got very close to God. He started telling me, through revelations, what He wanted me to do. He gave me his holy scriptures, the chapters, verses and all. Then He started telling me when to fast and pray. He directed me and led me in a very divine way. He gave me dreams and visions and success in my life. I was sick with many illnesses and He has healed, saved, blessed, and delivered me.

Today I have a total and completely clean bill of health.

I encourage you to get as close to God as you possibly can. Keep your family closely knit, stay in the word of God, fast and pray. Watch and pray and be sober and vigilant for God.   Ask God to increase your faith, wisdom, knowledge and understanding so you can fly as high and wide as the eagles. I will be praying on this end that God will give you grace, mercy and truth and also the fruits of the spirit. Talk to God everyday. Do not cease praying. Seek His face always.

Truly,

Sister Kate Randolph

Chapter Reflections

Introduction to Chapter 6

Dear _____,

Have you ever been blessed by a stranger? Well, that's what this chapter is all about. A stranger is someone we don't know but often they come to our aid bestowing gifts, wisdom, advice and help. Help that seems so personal and tailor made for us; it is as if they really do know us!

Elaine

Hebrews 13-2

...Don't forget to entertain strangers for by doing so some people have entertained angels without knowing it.

The Kindness of Strangers

Dear _____,

I first knew Mary as 'the blind woman" from church. I'd see her from time to time, walking up the aisle with her cane, or standing up at the lector stand, or I'd hear her voice when she cantered in the choir. I knew who she was but I didn't really know her.

One day after mass a group of people were standing outside the church and Mary was among them.

I began talking to a woman I knew who happened to be accompanying Mary. She had to leave suddenly and asked me if I would escort Mary over to the rectory, where they were having a celebration for one of the priests. I was a little reluctant, as I had never "taken care of" a blind person before, but I did.

As I walked over with her, I wondered what I would do when we got there. There would be food there, but how would she know what to eat, if she couldn't see it. I walked her over to the table, told her what foods they had, and fixed a plate for her and for myself.

It was an informal gathering, so we just stood around for a while. I felt awkward at first, because I didn't want to leave her, so I began talking with her.

I found out she did the same type of work that I did. She was a computer programmer. I was amazed.

Over the next several months, I began to see Mary often. At first, I just wanted to help her because I thought about how difficult it must be to be blind. But, Mary was incredibly independent. She managed to get back and forth to work, fix her own meals, do her own laundry, pay her own bills and even go grocery shopping on her own.

The more I got to know her I realized she did not want my help. All she really wanted was my friendship.

Now, Mary is no longer the "blind woman" from church. She is my friend.

We do things together just like any other friends. We go to eat, go shopping, have tea together, we go to concerts and plays and even watch movies.

Mary has taught me that people who have disabilities don't just need help. They also need friends.

Anonymous

Dear _____,

I bring you Blessings and Greetings in the name of our Lord and Savior, Jesus Christ.

It is a privilege to share my experience with you on how God will and shall provide all your needs according to his riches in Christ Jesus.

I thank God for using a woman named Judy to be a support and inspiration to me. I was and am a single woman with five children. When my children were small, my only source of income was 35.00 weekly. But, through God's grace and infinite mercy, he touched her heart JUST FOR ME.

My mother's friend worked for Judy as a babysitter for Judy's three children, who were about the same age as mine. This Jewish woman saw fit to share her children's clothing with me.

She would send bags of clothes with the tags still on them from stores like, Macy's, Jamboree and the Children's Place.

As a result of this my children were the best dressed in the church.

I give glory to the Father who loves me so much, despite the fact that it seemed like I wasn't going to make it. So, I pray as a single woman trusting in the Lord, that you will have faith and believe that he will make a way when there seems to be no way. God works in ways that we can't see. So, I say to you, just believe, just believe.

Sandy Durr

Dear _____,

I just wanted to take this opportunity to share with you how God can literally step into what seems to be an impossible situation.

It was a cold winter day. There wasn't much snow, but it sure was cold. I had just gotten off work and it was one of those days that I wanted to go home and kick back and relax. My girls were little then...if memory serves me right Brittany was eight years old and Cachet was six.

The girl's father, my boyfriend at the time, had picked me up from work to go and pick up the girls.

I got the girls and we proceeded to go home. I go up the stairs of my apartment and go in. I turn the light switch on and nothing happened. My heart started racing. I was afraid to think the worse. I looked outside to see if there was a power outage or if something had happened. No luck! Everything is working fine, except the power in my house.

The electricity had been shut off. I wanted to cry, but I couldn't show my girls that I was afraid and hurt. I had to show them that I was strong and that everything was okay. The girl's father went and got some ice so that the meat in the refrigerator could go in a cooler and stay cool until I could figure out what I needed to do. I lit some candles and went and got a change of clothes for the girls and myself, because we could not stay in the house.

I went to my mother's house. She was upset that the power was turned off, especially when I had two small children.

The next day, I was walking around in a daze. I just didn't know what to do. I was at work and I needed to make a decision.

I'll never forget. It was like it happened yesterday. I began to break down outside of the building where I worked. Then, all of a sudden this lady I had seen before, but didn't really know, asked me if everything was okay. I just broke down and told her what had happened. She was very understanding and compassionate. She was very calm and spoke very directly but with love in her voice.

She told me that I needed to go to the Department of Social Services where they help people who are in need or who have an emergency situation.

So, I calmed down and went upstairs and told my boss that I needed to leave work because I had to deal with an emergency situation. He seemed very understanding and said okay. I went down to Social Services. I was very afraid because I didn't know what they would say.

Well, I told them what had happened and they asked me for documentation; birth certificates, information about me and just about everything else they could ask— they did. They told me that before they could do anything they would need this documentation.

Well, thank you Jesus, the next morning, I went down there and gave them everything they asked for. The woman there made one call and my life had changed. She told me that the power would be on when I got home. Talk about God sending you an angel when you are in a dark place! YES, ONLY GOD CAN DO THAT! He used a stranger to give direction and until this day she is still one of my very best friends.

So, no matter what it looks like, God will always send just what you need for that particular situation.

Sister Areatha Bryant

Dear_____,

Life is a learning experience. We meet all kinds of people along the way. Some may tell us good things while others may say things that hurt us in some way. It is not always from the good that we gain our strengths, for each bad thing is a lesson learned and in learning the lesson we become stronger. I have also learned that while God has blessed us with family, He has also blessed us with strangers, and it's from a stranger I heard these words that turned my life around in a positive way.

I was about eleven years old when it was discovered that my "rudeness" was really a hearing impairment.

Upon this discovery, my life changed dramatically. For years, I was constantly taken from one doctor to the next, given hearing tests, and in the end I was fitted with a hearing aid. Good thing right?

Not so, for it is a hard thing when you are the only child in school with a hearing problem and have to walk around with earphone devices attached to your ears that were quite visible to anyone getting close enough to you.

I would rather not wear them than be teased or shut out from my close group of friends, and so I continued to strain my ears, barely grasping some of the lessons taught by my teachers to whom I was the most outstanding student in my class. I relied on my text books to "catch up" with what I missed in class. In order to pass spelling exams I would memorize all the words we would be tested on, this way when it was spoken I knew exactly what word my teacher was referring to when she called them out. Yes, I was very creative. And, that is how I have lived my life, by finding my way around the obstacles set before me.

Everyone has a breaking point and mine came when my school decided to have hearing tests done on all the students. I knew ahead of time what I was up against but I was not prepared for the effect it would have on me.

One by one, my classmates returned to class with smiles on their faces, soon it was my turn to take the test. I left the classroom knowing I would fail, I even told the audiologist doing the test, I was going to fail but she insisted I had to take it anyway.

The results were not good, neither was the expression on her face because she probably could not understand why a child so deaf was going to a regular school without hearing aids and such. So, she gave me this pitiful look and told me to return to class.

The look bothered me because I did not like to be pitied, so I returned to class with that look in my eyes trying to shake the whole thing off. As I returned to the classroom one of my friends called our "Hey Rhonda, did ya pass the hearing test?" I could not hold back any longer.

Tears that I held back during those years of testing and dealing with everyday life in general, flowed from my eyes. It was so bad my shoulders started shaking and I had to lean my head on my desk and shield myself from my classmates. My friend naturally felt bad. She came by my desk and said she was sorry. She didn't mean to make me cry, but that only made me cry harder.

The teacher continued to teach and to this day I cannot tell what the lesson was about because I was still crying. Class dismissed and I was still crying. It was then I felt a gentle shake on my shoulders. She gently lifted my hands and stared into my tear stained face.

Blue eyes met brown ones and then almost in a whisper but quite clear, I heard "GOD does not give you more than you can handle. He has blessed you because despite your disability you are the top student in your class". She said so much more but those two sentences are the words I held on to.

After those words, I picked myself up and was able to make it through the rest of the day and other days that followed. I call her a stranger because I did not know her before she came to my school to teach and that was my final year in that school, so I never saw her after graduation. We only had one brief encounter to say good-bye to each other, never to see each other again. Her name was Ms. Santos and she made a tremendous difference in my life.

Rhonda Baird

Dear_____,

It was a very busy shift at work that day. The hustling kind when you're buried in work because you are steadily giving your all, completing one task while adding 3 or more to the agenda. Yet, I managed to get things done while breathing a deep sign of relief as I caught up. Meanwhile, one of my patients, using his call light was asking for an analgesic.

It was five minutes before clock out time. I was hesitant and my thoughts were to leave this task for the next shift nurse. Furthermore, his room was a distance. However, compassion filled me because Mr. Brant was a diabetics, had an amputation below the knee and (the stump incision was not healing) necrotic left toes (with the prognosis of amputation) heart failure, dialysis three times a week, bruised right finger and he was severely hard of hearing.

Besides, I told myself it would only take a few seconds to give the pain pill to him. Well, upon entering his room, I stood at his bedside. Suddenly, Mr. Brant started to sing. He was singing to me making direct eye contact. I informed him that I had medication for his discomfort, but he did not reach for the pills. He continued singing with a big smile on his face. Mr. Brant had made a comment during the earlier part of my shift about how busy the staff seemed and now here he was consoling me with a song.

Even though his tone was way off key, it was soothing to hear after a stressful day. I did not interrupt and he finished the song. I gave him the analgesic and clocked out with a smile. This day was worthwhile. Mr. Brandt made it rewarding.

Sincerely,

Rhonda Green

Chapter Reflections

Introduction to Chapter 7

Dear _____,

If you're a woman you have been blessed with so many gifts.

You are courageous, wise, compassionate, beautiful, persistent, self less— the list just goes on and on!

We women have been blessed to be multi-taskers and many times we are the ones standing in the gap for our families and patching up the holes in our communities. We make the way possible for so many others. Without women the world would cease to exist! The letters in this chapter should encourage you and let you know that you are not alone WOMAN. They should also remind you that you are needed and appreciated and when we take one step for the cause of others, we will be rewarded because now someone else will be able to take two steps, three steps, and another, and another and another until they reach their goal. We help others to dream, to try, to live their best lives. You and countless others are doing amazing things in towns, cities, villages and countries throughout the world. Yes, indeed a hand that rocks a cradle also "creates" a world.

Elaine

Isaiah 58-10

...and if you open yourself in behalf of the hungry and satisfy the needs of the oppressed, then your light will rise in the darkness...

A Hand That Rocks A Cradle, Also Creates A World

Jeremiah 29:11 - For surely I know the plans I have for you says God, plans for your welfare and not for harm, to give you a future with hope. Then when you call upon me and come and pray to me, I will hear you. When you search for me you will find me, if you seek me with all your heart I will let you find me.....

Dear_____,

How powerful these words were to me when I first began discerning my call to religious life and how powerful they remain as my journey with the Sisters of Mercy continues.

As a single mother of two sons I began to realize more than ever how important my faith was to me. I returned to teaching when my marriage ended in 1981. I felt lost and a bit scared as I reentered the workplace. I chose to return to a Catholic school for that is where I had taught before my children were born. This opportunity also enabled me to gain some self confidence, a skill of mine which needed some work.

During this time many people came into my life and supported me and it was just what I needed. As I taught the second graders in my class I was always touched with the wonder and awe that they displayed in all that was presented to them especially as we talked about God. It was tough making ends meet but the boys and I did it and life went on.

When the boys reached their teenage years, they felt very drawn to have more of a relationship with their father. When they decided to go live with their father I was devastated. I will always remember my oldest son telling me, "Mom, this will give you an opportunity to move on with your life." Was this tough? Yes, but I realize now that it was an opportunity for me to be open to where God was calling me.

One of the images that I have come to reflect on as my journey continues is the image of a door closing only to reveal another door opening. The newly opened doors have given me opportunities to grow in ways I never thought possible. The emptiness I felt when the boys went to live with their father helped me to look deep within myself and discover what areas of my life I needed to work on and then to be open to what God was calling me to do. Was it hard? Yes, but the best part is realizing how everything has fallen into place.

Entering a community of religious women has been rewarding and challenging. I have been given numerous opportunities to grow and to meet so many wonderful women. I have also been given opportunities to reflect on my life, to strengthen my relationship with God and to take steps that I never thought I would be able to take.

When people see me now they comment, "Barbara I have never seen you look so happy and so at peace," I hadn't heard this in a long time. My journey with the Sisters of Mercy has enabled me to accept who I am and discover the peace that is so necessary when one wants to move forward.

I think women need to take time for themselves. They need to be willing to accept feeling empty at times; sitting with that emptiness and being open to what adventures will be revealed to them.

I am grateful to all who continue to support me as my journey continues. I am most thankful to my children, Christopher and Matthew, to my brothers and my sister, my friends and most especially to the Sisters of Mercy.

I will never forget the day of my mother's funeral, right after I had entered. My cousin and I were walking out of the church and she told me how happy she was for me. I was surprised for I hadn't told too many people about my decision to enter. I thanked her and commented I wasn't sure of what my mother thought, my cousin said, "Barbara the last time I was with your mother she shared with me your decision to enter. She wanted you to marry a rich man and when I commented Aunt Anna, she did meet a rich man. My mother said, "Yes, she did, didn't she!" What better affirmation could I have had?

I feel honored that I have been able to share my journey with you and I pray that all who read this will be open to all that could unfold for them.

In Mercy,

Sr. Barbara Quinn

Dear _____,

I want to ask you a question? If you awoke one morning and saw thick black smoke billowing from the roof of your neighbor's home, would you run, to their house, beat on the door, bang on the windows and yell to the top of your voice to try and awake the sleeping occupants and make sure they got out of that burning house safely?

If you saw a little child run from behind a parked car, into the street and into the path of an oncoming car, would you instantly, without thinking, run after him to save him from being hit.

Most of us, if we were face to face with these scenarios would probably respond.

But, many times the challenges stopping us from helping someone are not that life threatening, not that dire, and not that dangerous to our own personal health, yet we refuse to get involved.

The little boy who rides the school bus with your child, doesn't wear socks to school in the dead of winter. When you hear that, does that bother you? The girls who live in the group home down the street, will not be receiving presents or visits during the holidays from their biological families. Did you know that?

Those senior citizens who sit outside on the lawn of the nursing home, and watch you as you drive by never get a letter or visitor. What do you think of that?

What I'm asking is who have you helped lately? Whose life have you changed? What have you done with your talents, gifts? Or are you too busy waiting for that knight in shining armor to come along. Or, working those three jobs to buy that fancy home on the hill so you can get away from it all? Well, I've got news for you the world is waiting on you. Kids are crying for you and people are dying out there; waiting to get their hands on that thing you refuse to part with. That thing is your talent, your gift, your way of doing things that will make the world a better place. But, you're too caught up in YOURSELF to see what's going on.

The reason I sat to write you this letter is because I was gearing up for my annual after school reading program. It's called 'The Cookie House." Usually, I work with two schools and I take ten kids from each school.

I have five or six volunteers and we tutor and encourage these kids. They are some of the sweetest kids and when I look at them I always see promise in their eyes. This year, I received applications for 50 kids and it just broke my heart! Because I knew I only had 6 volunteers and with this lopsided equation there was no way I could help all the kids, kids who so desperately needed the help. Now, I would have to choose who got into the program and who did not. Some would now have to be put on a waiting list and the wait would last forever because you were not around. I was upset because I was wondering where you were and why you were not lending a hand.

Where are the people who could be helping our kids? Where are the people who should be helping our kids? What are you doing with your life while a child waits for you?

If you were thinking, someone else would take your place, you were wrong. Your place is vacant. There are no replacements. There are no reinforcements.

And what about you woman? Are you so caught up in clothes and nails and hair and your emotions that you don't dare to step in and be a friend to someone in need. This letter is for you!

Not having enough time isn't an excuse either because time is the same for everybody. You have only 24 hours and so do I. The smart businesswoman, or the A student, or that volunteer who always seems to be able to help so many people, they are no smarter than you, its what they do with their 24 hours that makes them more efficient.

As women, we can change the status quo. It is in us to achieve great things on the behalf of others. The letters in this book prove that real power lies within us. Put women together to do a task and it gets done and everyone is enriched. No one is left out or overlooked or dismissed. We change the world! But, to do that we will have to change some of our priorities, figuratively clean out our "closets" and throw away the things that don't fit. We'll have to choose more mean-ingful projects that leave us feeling fulfilled as well as the recipient.

OK, I know I'm preaching here, but I have to. I speak to groups a lot and this is the same message I give them. USE YOUR LIFE FOR THE GOOD OF OTHERS! Live your life! Don't just exist.

No woman is an island, and yes! I am my brother's and sister's keeper so why aren't you doing "great" big things or "great" little things to help someone in need? Woman, it is in you! What "great thing" do you have within your power to do for someone else?

Would you just start off by buying an extra pair of socks and tell your child to "discreetly" give them to the child with no socks? Would you save money, a little of your allowance and buy Christmas presents and drop them off anonymously at the group home? Would you call the nursing home and ask if you could befriend one of the elderly residents or start a pen pal relationship?

The bottom line is that this is your watch. This is the era you were born, the time that you are alive. How will you give an account of your time?

Ok, I've preached and yelled at you enough. But, here's one final thought.

How far would you go to help someone in need? If "you" were that someone in need, how far would you want someone to go for you?

Elaine Houston

Dear _____,

I am very fortunate to have the opportunity, through my work, to make a difference in the lives of girls in our community. The positive power of my contribution often gets lost in the struggles and challenges I experience in running a non-profit organization, especially in these turbulent times. But, here they continue to come, these girls, to be supported in their goals, to be encouraged to reach further for their dreams and to choose wisely by the committed and talented staff I work with at Girls Incorporated. They are the reminders, the touchstones, if you will, of why I have continued along this path these past fourteen years.

When I lose sight of the "big picture" because of a fiscal challenge I am working overtime to overcome for example, and begin to feel overwhelmed, along comes one of the girls, with "her story". Inevitably, her story is so compelling, her need for our encouraging environment so great, that I get reinvigorated and tackle that challenge with a renewed sense of urgency and an even stronger commitment to the mission and vision of the work.

The rate of burn out in this field is pretty high. The research tells us that Executive Directors and CEO's don't typically take another position as head of an organization once they leave. It is certainly understandable! The pressures are tremendous, the responsibilities huge, the workday is long and erratic and the challenges endless. The pay is often low and the standards "perks" are left to our corporate, for-profit counterparts.

However, in this line of work, the perks are of a different variety. The work is connected to changing girls' lives, for the better. Seeing a girl graduate from high school, be the first in her family to go to college, become a US Navy Rescue Swimmer, graduate from Harvard School of Law, reach her goal, whatever that may be, these are the perks of this work.

The mission of our organization is to inspire all girls to be strong, smart and bold (c) however, in the final analysis, it is the girls who provide me the inspiration to get up in the morning, approach my work as the gift that it truly is and experience a deep sense of gratitude for being included in their lives. Thank you for inviting me to stop and consider this aspect of my life.

Teri Bordenave

Dear_____,

One night I was watching one of those so-called "reality" shows. I don't watch them often because I don't think they portray "reality" at all. But, this one I liked. It was called "The Apprentice" and that mega gazillionaire, Donald Trump was the CEO of the show. Each week he gave 12 young, enthusiastic, entrepreneurial up and comers an assignment. They worked in teams, men against the women. The group that trumped the other, (no pun intended) moved closer to running a real business for Donald Trump, making real money.

On this night, the genders were mixed and the group I liked was struggling. The leader, a young woman, discovered as they were counting up the day's receipts, that the group had somehow lost nearly two hundred dollars. She decided when the group came before Trump in the boardroom, she as the leader would take the blame for the loss. I thought that showed character and true leadership ability. Wait, I'm getting ahead of myself! I should tell you that when a losing team met with Trump the leader had to sacrifice two teammates whom he or she thought aided in the loss. (The goal was to narrow the field, so there would only be one eventual winner.

So, when the leader met with Trump she brought along two of her teammates. Trump asked the two women to explain themselves and they without hesitation, defended themselves to the finish, fighting tooth and nail not to be fired. For her part, the leader did as she said and accepted the blame for the loss. Again, I thought that was good enough to secure her spot but to my dismay Donald Trump fired her! I was shocked until he gave the reason for his decision. He said he fired the young lady because she didn't fight, didn't stand up for herself.

I pondered his decision, asking myself "Why would he fire her?" As the show went off, I finally I got it! Taking the blame was the right thing to do, it's the action of a good leader but she should have backed up her decision. Leaders fight and are respected for doing so. She went down without a fight. You can never give up the fight. You know, many women give up the fight in the business world. The reasons for this are varied.

Sometimes, its because for so long men were the only ones sitting behind the CEO desk and we as women, deferred to them. Oftentimes, we run into the glass ceiling, and we're so tired from the climb, we give up, thinking it is impossible to ever make it to the top. But, ladies, things are changing and if we are going to be in a position to make an impact on the lives of many people, we must fight.

Now, I must caution you there are consequences to standing up for yourself. At times the consequences are painful but standing up and speaking up for myself is a decision I've made. I finally know who I am and I know that I was created to change the world, in my own small way. When I stand up for myself, I'm also standing up for those whose lives I will affect. If I don't succeed they will not succeed.

I remember a time when I stood up for myself. I was working at a television station and contract time was nearing.   I hated contract time because no matter how well I did, no matter how great the ratings were, no matter how great my public approval rating was, my raise was never commensurate with my achievements.

I always left the talks feeling I'd been taken advantage of. So, I agonized the upcoming meeting.

 In fact, I was angry and I said to God, I don't want to do this, you know what will happen. "What do you want?" HE said. I took out a piece of paper and I wrote down the things I wanted. All the while, I talked to God. After numbering my list, I went back — across from my desires I wrote down what I had done to earn each request. I talked about all I'd done in helping the company succeed. I also mentioned the things I'd done in my community and I wrote down scriptures of God's promises to me. And, I made a pact with God that I would trust HIM to get the things I wanted in my contract for me. I would not even consider or put the decision in the hands of management. I would trust in God because I believed God loved me. I believed that GOD was more powerful in this matter than I was.

The day of the talks, I went in and I listened and the offer was better than I thought it would be. I wasn't becoming rich, but my raise was a little higher than normal. I told management I needed a day to get back to them about the offer. I walked out smiling thinking O-K this is OK! That's when I heard this small, small voice inside me says, "But that is not what you said you wanted." Oh!!!!!!!!! Please, please don't remind me of that, I thought. I heard it again, "But that is not what you said you wanted." This contract sounds ok. I pleaded. "But, that is not what you said you wanted, I heard again." "OK", I said." " I'll stick to our agreement, I said."

The next day I went back and told them I was refusing the contract. I told them what I really wanted and they said "NO". I kept my pact and management kept away from me; ostracized me. I did a lot of praying to God and I did a lot of crying. I told God I should have accepted that contract. HE told me to trust HIM. It was a lesson in standing up for myself. Whenever I complained, God gave me his word, Jeremiah 29-11 "For I know the plans I have for you, to prosper you not to harm you."

Nine months later, I received the raise I had asked for. I celebrated. I had learned the lesson of standing up for myself in the face of tremendous odds.

Elaine Houston

Chapter Reflections

Introduction to Chapter 8

Dear_____,

When's the last time you laughed until your sides hurt? Sometimes, we as women are so busy being the mother, father, career woman, bread winner, homework helper, the plumber, the laundry lady, you get the picture; that we forget that there is also a time to laugh. Do it with me right now, JUST LAUGH OUT LOUD. Keep going! Didn't that feel good? Whew! Ok, let me compose myself.!!!! The following letters are intended to remind you to include fun in you life. Take time out for yourself. You may have to pencil it in your appointment book, or write it down on your calendar. You deserve it and as one letter proves even a shopping trip can turn into a laugh a minute.

Elaine

Proverbs 17:22

...a cheerful heart is good medicine but a crushed spirit dries up the
bones.

A Girl Just Wants To Have A Little Fun

Dear _____,

Today, I arrived at the office at 7:00am, prepared for volunteer meetings by 8:00AM, accomplished several customer meetings by 12:00 noon, helped a friend rewrite a resume, provided support to my staff regarding professional issues, made some money for the company by 6:00 pm, then ran to the store between my next meeting to buy a pogo stick for my 12 year old son, Ben, and continued on my way to an evening Board Meeting. As I pulled in the driveway tonight, I smiled knowing that girls' weekend was 10 days away! I wondered if I should have bought the hoola hoops for the girls. Yes, Thank goodness we have scheduled another—girls' weekend!

It all started sixteen years ago, a childhood friend called finding herself alone with a drama unfolding. She was faced with a personal decision about whether to stay with her husband of 10 years. Because she had children and she was feeling overwhelmed with moving forward she called in a panic to see if I could meet her in neutral place away from our homes. I dropped everything and flew from New York and she flew from California within a day. She felt she was falling apart. We met in the Chicago airport. We embraced as if time had never passed and vowed that we would never let so much time pass without a hug, a laugh or simple sharing.

We spent those evenings together eating, drinking strawberry daiquiris looking at pictures of our families.

Of course the weekend was filled with shopping at an outlet that distracted my friend in between facing her deep sadness. The pedicures side by side sent us laughing recalling memories of our childhood.

I think this was the weekend where I realized that girlfriends are about sharing life, having fun and creating adventures. It is about the meaningful moments when facing responsibilities and decisions that seem too large to bear, where you can reach out and receive support. This girls' weekend was not meant to solve a challenge but to remind us each to keep sharing our experiences together, sustaining friendship in our lives even during the most challenging events and not to forget to laugh together.

In our parting, going back to our lives, we promised to meet every year in a different city, in a different state, scheduling a massage and a manicure, every year for the rest of our lives. This year, we will be visiting our 16ᵗʰ state, sharing photos of our families, a massage and a pedicure, of course.

This weekend experience created a continued commitment to myself to live, love and laugh out loud with my girlfriends in all aspects of my life.

The girlfriend moments that forever leave me with a smile are:

- Snow tubing down a hill with 6 women, screaming and laughing and barely catching our breaths.
- Coordinating a reading group for sharing life's experiences and sharing our favorite foods.
- Preparing a community Thanksgiving dinner with a group of vegetarians, cutting up turkey giblets for gravy...nothing goes to waste!
- Sitting in a hot tub, watching the moon cross the sky, laughing about each other's short comings.
- Venturing on a skiing weekend when you don't ski but know how to cook and select a few good wines!
- Sliding into 1000 galloons of cold, wet, slimy red jello to raise money for a local non-profit.
- A perennial exchange, book swap, or clothing and jewelry trade.
- Collecting funds for a non-for-profit that provides services to women and women with children.
- Slumber party, Twister, story telling and listening to the Four Tops
- Goal setting at a small café' drinking a Chai tea, every two months revisiting where we are.
- Soccer mom investment club...invest some money, share mom stories and sip coffee
- And, finally dreaming while walking through the streets of Florence sharing travel adventures. Having a group of women friends has pulled me through good times and challenging times. I encourage women to make time together to share, support each other, be a girl and create opportunities to just have some fun. Thoughts, emotions, moods come and go, memories of laughter are what get us through each day.

Positively,

Beth Coco

Dear_____,

Some of the best times I've had in my life have been on shopping trips with my girlfriends.

One, in particular was a trip to Manchester, Vermont with my friend Carolyn. Neither of us had much money. I had 100.00. I think she had about the same, maybe a little bit more.

But, we needed to get away from Albany, New York, where we lived and Manchester was just far enough away to make you feel as though you had gotten away. In Manchester, there are a number of designer outlet stores and there's no rule that you have to be rich to shop in Manchester but invariably whenever I go there, I always see people who look and act as if they belong on "Lifestyles of the Rich and Famous".

Anyway, having $100.00 to $150.00 was just not enough for you buy much in Manchester at the outlets, but on this day, we were going more for the atmosphere, the clear sky, the window shopping and maybe we had enough money to buy lunch and a scarf or something.

But, it cost nothing to look! So, look we did, and let me tell you the clothes there are SO NICE! You just felt like having one of everything. You become a glutton- wanting everything you saw.

But, we were wise shoppers. We could afford one item but it had to be the right item.

So, we kept looking. Store after store, we oooed and ah-h-h-hed at the beautiful silks but we could not afford anything. Then, we decided to forgo the clothes and try shoes. I wear an 11aa, so I didn't expect to find anything, but Carolyn wears a nine or nine 1/2, so like a good friend, I accompanied her, scouting shoes just for her. Down one aisle and up the next we went, searching the racks. That's when I heard it, G-U-R-R-R-L! I knew it was pay dirt but I wasn't quite sure just how big of a find she'd made. I followed the wailing until I got to her and I immediately looked down at her feet and then our eyes met and simultaneously, we yelled G-U-R-R-R-R-R-L! We were like a two ten year old girls, with braces, squealing over a magazine cover of our favorite teen idol. "Girl, those are bad, you have to get them, how much are they, they'll go with everything, people will be so jealous of you, I screamed!" Now, let me pause here. When you find a pair of shoes that are that bad, even though they are not for you, you scream in appreciation—

because you are so happy for your friend. Women do that! It's just a girl thing! (Men, I'm sure don't squeal over a pair of Stacy Adams.) There is no jealousy (ok, maybe a little) because just to be seen with your friend wearing those shoes somehow makes you look good too!

These shoes were black and silver stripes. They had a 3-inch heel, with a pointed toe and black strap around the heel. They were satin evening shoes and they looked like they were 6 or 7 hundred dollars. I mean they looked expensive! Carolyn has very shapely legs and she just looked great in them. Did I say they looked like they cost about 6 or 7 hundred dollars. Well, we got them for under 80.00, YES!!!

Now, it was my turn and I could see in my sister's eyes that she wanted me to find something great too. But, it would have to be clothes. There would be no shoes for me today. So, we hit all the shops on one side of the street and decided to try the shops on the other side. We hadn't gone long before we stopped in a shop that caught my eye. We went immediately to the sale rack and there I found an ice blue, spaghetti strapped, beaded camisole thingy. I continued my search and found an emerald green, Linda Allard, Ellen Tracy, silk blouse. It was a size 8. I wear a size 10 but as my momma always says you get what you pay for and this expensive blouse in size 8 fit my size 10 body for $45.00.

The searched continued until I came across a black wrap that you could wear over an evening dress. It was sans collar and was held together by a clasp at the neck and on my 5' 10" frame it looked lovely. So, I got it! My total bill was $136.00. Carolyn spotted me for the $36.00 (which I paid once we got home) and now it was time for a little dessert!

We bought our cookies and soda and started our trek back to Albany. But, we were going back feeling refreshed. With the sun roof open on her Lexus, we laughed about our fabulous purchases, sang to the music on the CD player and felt all was right with the world!

Elaine Houston

Dear _____,

My most exciting time I had with a girlfriend was when we went from St. Louis, Missouri to Niagara Falls, NY.

From St. Louis, we headed to South Bend, Indiana. When we arrived, I met all my girlfriend's kinfolks-beautiful people. We had dinner, toured the city, visited more relatives and then got a good night sleep.

The next morning we had a big breakfast before hitting the expressway for Detroit, Michigan.

We arrived in Detroit in the late afternoon, found a hotel and dropped off our bags. I called a friend who lived there. She joined us and gave us a tour of the "Motor City". Later, we all returned to the hotel took a shower and put on our Sunday best because we were ready to roll.

We dined at the fabulous Renaissance Center; a revolving dining room where we had dinner and drinks, with a view of two lakes. My friend from Detroit took us to several other hot spots, the East side, the West Side. By this time it was getting late and it was all started to look alike.

The next morning, we said goodbye to our Detroit friend and it was on the road to Canada.

We checked into a hotel in Toronto, Canada that afternoon and rested until it was time to go to dinner. We had dinner in our hotel and learned there was a band playing downstairs. We decided to see what the Canadians were playing so we went downstairs and through a door that we thought was leading to where the music was playing. As we continued down the stairs we met a woman who was motioning to us and saying something to us. We passed by her and continued heading down the steps until we hit a dead end.   We turned around and headed back up. Finally, it dawned on us the lady was telling us we were going the wrong way. But, she was speaking French and of course we didn't speak French. We started laughing!

The next morning after breakfast we went shopping; great shopping and then we had lunch at the top of the luxurious CN tower. After lunch, we hit the road for Niagara Falls, we got lost a few times but finally we arrived at the Falls, had dinner and went as close as we could to watch the Falls as the lights changed. It was such a beautiful sight.

156

The next morning after breakfast, we went shopping for souvenirs and went to a bowling tournament before heading home. Now that was a fun trip full of excitement.

Liz

Dear _____,

One of the best times I had was with my friend I met while working in Kalamazoo, Michigan, quite possibly the coldest spot in the world, second only to Albany, New York.

Her name is Marci Jones. I call her Marci bird. She's a teeny-tiny little thing with a huge personality. Anytime with her, I knew would be fun. This day was no exception.

We started out wanting to go, let me rephrase that, with Marci wanting us to go biking on one of the precious few sunny days of the year. I didn't have a bike, so she brought her old one for me to use.

It looked like it was plucked right out of a Norman Rockwell painting; the square seat, rusty chain, huge pedal, three speeds. Next, to Marci's mountain bike, it clunked. I was grateful anyway and we started out.

It was so hot and the physical activity kicked up the temperature. But, we had a goal, after all. The promise land came in the form of a sundae shoppe called Treat Street.

Once there, we felt we deserved the gold medal,"the Piglet." A mound of ice cream as
big as your head with ooey-gooey topping, whipped cream, you name it.

We sat there with Piglets insight, spoons in hand and ate until we were sick. In between bites we would smile for the picture we thought they should put up of us in the shoppe for finishing our Piglets. The site of her with that hot-fudge covered grin made me snort like a piglet, choking on my ice cream. A sweet memory for a sweet time.

Karen Lehane

Chapter Reflections

Introduction to Chapter 9

Dear _____,

Where would we be without our mothers and sisters? They are the first female friends in our lives. When was the last time you spoke to your mom or hugged your sister? They've taught you so much.

Now, it's your turn to pay tribute to them. In this chapter, make sure you read the touching tribute from a daughter to a mother who has just passed away. Also read about the life of Miss Willie Mae, a true renaissance woman from Shabuta, Miss.

If you are not close to your mom or sister, there is still time. Resolve your differences, tell her you love her and start to live a remarkable life.

Elaine

Genesis 12-11

...I know what a beautiful woman you are.

Luke 11-27

...Blessed is the mother who gave you birth.

My Sister, My Friend, My Mother, Myself

Dear _____,

If you look at me, you're also looking at my mother. I look just like her, from the thick hair, to the high cheekbones, to the eyes. I am my mother's child. Get this- I even sound like her! Its true, I catch myself talking and notice that my voice, (the tone and sound) sounds just like mama!

Isn't that funny? To me its funny because when I was younger I never noticed it but, the older I get I see more of my mom in me. At 67 or is it 68, my mom looks like she is in her 50's and she dresses nicely and still has it going on! You're reading my mind aren't you? Yes, I hope I look as good as she does when I'm her age.

But, as much as I take after my mother physically, the attribute I love most is my mom's character.

She's honest, she's giving, she is kind. If I'm going down the wrong path, she'll say, "You shouldn't do that." I still address her with "yes ma'am or no ma'am ". I respect her and she respects me. When I complain to her about my enemies, she says, "Pray for them". She's a virtuous woman.

While, she 's always pushed her kids to be independent, I know that I can always go back home.

My mom is also my best friend. She encourages me and supports my ideas and on many occasions she's told me she's proud of me. I have done the same for her.

I thank God that my mom is in good health and every year, we take a trip together overseas. We have a great time!!!

I am very aware that I am blessed to have a relationship like this because I know there are many people who aren't welcomed back home. I know there are many people at odds with their mother and who haven't spoken to her in years. Have my mother and I disagreed? Absolutely, but we know how to forgive and forget. I also know that my mom wouldn't deliberately try and harm me, so I tell myself that it's okay, if we don't see eye to eye. There's nothing more important than me getting back in a right relationship with her. You see, I'm not sure if she'll be with me the next day, so I treasure each day like it's our last together.

Elaine Houston

Dear_____,

Mom, just when I thought I had lost you forever, Toni Morrison, the great African American author, through her writings and teachings, convinced me that I could and should continue to communicate with you even though you have been dead for more than thirty years.

After all, you were the one who taught me the major personal and moral values that I live by. You were my role model, closest friend and most loyal confidant.

So, at this juncture in my life, I want to review with you some of the most important decisions I have made in my life and ponder whether they measure up to your teachings, values, and hopes. Like you, there are children, grandchildren, and others who look to me for the same kind of guidance and direction you gave me. I want to serve them well.

First of all, I recall the enormous value you placed on all human life and individual freedom. This belief was most probably nurtured by your grandmother, Cicely Cawthon. She was born enslaved in 1859 and she raised you. Often, you mentioned her expressed outrage at being owned like property. And, she shared with you, her parent's tactics of resistance and survival with dignity. These were lessons sandwiched in between her cooking lessons and disciplining of you.

Although literacy was forbidden for those enslaved at the time, you reported that Great Grandmother Cawthon understood the value of education, which she instilled in you. In turn, you taught me how education could be used to improve one's lot in life, help others and promote the freedom of Black people. It was, according to you, a glorious gift, one that could not be taken away like liberty or property.

Thank goodness you lived long enough to see me become an educator. I will always remember your round brown face beaming with pride when you visited me at my first teaching job in an urban school. You saw that I took my assignment seriously and was able to empathize with my students whose lives were shaped by poverty and neglect.

For we too, had been poor.

My compassion took me beyond the classroom and into the homes and communities of my students. Their lives were often fractured, families split apart, housing in disrepair, and health care needs unmet.

165

In turn, these conditions made me feel angry and powerless yet prompted my determination to find ways to promote needed social change.

Then, I made the difficult decision to leave education, a judgment you might have seriously questioned since you realized the desperate need (that still exists) for black teachers in urban schools. But, I elected to pursue a career as a social worker and community organizer, believing that this would be the best way for me to help low-income people gain the political power needed to change oppressive social policies.

My timing was great! The War on Poverty was underway and community organizing strategies in Albany's South End were proving effective. Employed by a youth and family services center, I got into the thick of educating and organizing welfare recipients and community groups to demand better services, housing, recreation, education, jobs and the vote. Although this was the North, many people of color were not allowed to freely vote.

While my organizing work on the streets proved rewarding, I soon witnessed with great alarm, the horrifying injustices taking place in our criminal justice system. Many people of color both the South End and Arbor Hill sections of Albany, NY were routinely mistreated, criminalized and beaten by police officers with impunity. White courtrooms stepped up their sentencing of young blacks to jails and to prisons, as a vicious "war on drugs" was unleashed throughout the land. It was during this time of the late 70s that I became eager to learn much more about this "system of justice" that I found so disturbing and frightening. It was already apparent that imprisonment could be used to permanently block educational and employment opportunities for masses of people, destroy families, and disenfranchise and further impoverish large segment of African American communities.

Fearing the encroaching reach of the criminal justice system and prisons and their power to control and destroy lives, I decided to better prepare myself to meet the approaching challenge. This led to my enrollment in the criminal justice doctoral program at the University At Albany, where four years later, I earned my degree in 1982.

During my graduate studies I had been introduced to state prisons and given the wonderful opportunity to work with prisoners, most of whom had lived in poverty, were marginalized by racism, attended inferior urban schools and had found escape and opportunities only through illicit drugs. Many of them, I found, were bright and articulate critical thinkers who added immeasurably to my criminal justice education.

They viewed and understood the criminal justice system from a totally different perspective than that of academia. Their analysis, based on study and first hand experience, recognized the interrelatedness of history, race, crime, economics and politics, society's challenge, they argued, was to empower prisoners and others to take control of their lives through education, training, employment, and alternative treatment and activism in their own communities.

Much of my life over the past twenty years has been devoted to working with prisoners and educating those on the outside about the devastating costs of mass incarceration, racism, and the policies of disinvestments in communities of color. There are, I believe, significant similarities between the slavery of your grandmother's day and the prison system of today. Both have operated to devastate families and control and oppress people of color.

Mom, you and Great Grandmother Cawthon, serve to remind me that we must learn more from our ancestors and rethink our history so that we can recognize how they can help us adopt more critical and useful postures towards the present and the future.
I treasure all that you gave me and continue to give me.

Your loving daughter, Alice.

Alice Green

Dear_____,

I have had several deep and important friendships with women that have enriched my life immensely. I have almost always had a "best friend", but the one I never imagined would be closest to my heart is my sister Cathy. Cathy is four years younger than I, and my opposite in temperament and behavior. I was dramatic, tempestuous, intensely curious (nosy), rebellious, passionate, opinionated, quick to anger and fighting, and a thorn in my mother's side due to all of the above - not an easy child to have as your firstborn.

Cathy, who is third out of a total of eight was also passionate and feisty, but learned early on to temper it with calmness and patience, and the willingness to think about the feelings of others. She was smart and thoughtful, and an "A" student, star athlete, popular with the "good" kids, and someone my mother could be very proud of. We despised each other. I thought she was a "goody two-shoes", she thought me a ridiculous "rebel without a cause." We were both right.

Somehow, though, in her second year of college, under end-of-semester pressure from both deadlines and her own insistence on perfection, Cathy called ME for support. To this day, I'm not sure if either of us knows why she chose to call me, except that she knew that I would probably be comfortable with imperfection. With that phone call, however, she extended an olive branch across the turbulent waters of our relationship, a gift forever cherished by her older sister.

That was twenty-two years ago, and our friendship has grown and changed much over the years. We lived in the same neighborhood for nearly seven years, several blocks apart. When either of us came home after a bad day or just needed a sympathetic ear, we would pick up the phone and agree to meet halfway between our houses at the corner. In the dark, rain, snow, anytime at all, we would meet, hug, and walk and talk until whatever troubled us had uncoiled itself and we were at peace. We have walked and talked through all the joys and challenges life had offered each of us, through relationships starting and ending, adolescent children, career ups and downs, family illnesses—life's whole gamut.

In 1999, Cathy, in a move uncharacteristic for someone as deliberate and careful as she, took a leave of absence from her job, put all her stuff in storage, bought a four-wheel drive vehicle and a tiny trailer, and took off to explore the Southwest. The night before she left, she practiced backing up the trailer for hours, never quite getting the hang of it, and for the next three months she spent on the road, choosing only campsites, she could pull into.

She settled and has lived in Santa Fe for the past three years, a lovely place where I have enjoyed visiting her. A long way, though to be able to pick up the phone and say, "Meet me at the corner in ten minutes."

Lois Johnson

Dear _____,

Mom, I want you to know what a blessing you are to me. When I found out I was going to have a baby, you were not the first to know. You didn't take the news very well. I was still in school, I didn't have a good job, I wasn't in a position to have a baby and raise it on my own.

So, what you did is greatly appreciated. You invited me into your home with open arms. You provided my every meal and you never missed a doctor's appointment with me. Thank you.

You prayed for me day in and day out and now I am living the answered prayer! I thank you and I thank God for you. I love you.

Your daughter,

Audrey Baird

Dear _____,

I am the oldest of three children. Growing up in a single parent home was not always easy; never really understanding why mom did or said the things she did. But, as the second of nine children growing up in the South, her life was not always pleasant.

I would often wonder, "Where is my father," but I was afraid to ask. He was never spoken of and I wondered why he wasn't a part of my life. There's a scripture in the Bible that says, "When I was a child, I spoke as a child, but when I became a man (woman), I put away childish things.

I was a just a child, when I questioned those things.

We may have not spoken about matters of her heart, but she set a good example for me in so many ways. Now that I'm an adult woman, I'm proud to say, "Thank you God," for allowing me to grow up in a home where my mom worked everyday and I always had food, clothing and shelter. In fact, dinner was always cooked by 3:30 p.m. My mom was hardworking, and determined to build a future for her children. She did that by precept and example.

Now, that I am raising 8 children, I know that being a product of the good environment that I was raised in was a good thing.

Thank you mom, Jean Terry, (also known as Gobbie) for being a good example.

Shelly Ford

Dear_____,

I love my sister Wanda Fay. She is a very intelligent and articulate woman. She is always able to get her point across with precision. She has regal beauty that commands attention when she enters a room. I love her protective nature towards family and friends alike. She is like a lioness watching over her baby cubs.

She is an extraordinarily anointed musical director-teacher. She is able to bring out the full musical talent in an individual and musical group. Her accomplishments are many. After losing an election for a seat on the city council she remained focused to make a difference in her community and ran for office of county legislator. She Won!

 She is a champion for the sometimes misunderstood and hurting people in the community. She strives to keep our people productive and empowered. She was the first to recognize my musical talents and she has always encouraged me in my musical career. She helped me believe in my gifts. I will be forever grateful to her for giving me my wings to fly musically. She has blessed my life by being my sister, my friend, my coach and cheerleader. She is a Champion!

Barbara Howard

Dear_____,

My sister Barbara dares to dream. She dares to believe in her God-given gift and talent and passionately pursues it. Growing up the youngest of seven siblings has its ups and downs. In your younger years you are treated special. You are the "baby" and being the baby of the family has its privileges. You have a tendency to get your way. You are assigned the least amount of work to do in the house. You are Daddy's favorite and nobody is jealous. The down side to being the "baby sister" is that no one will let you grow up.
You are married for 17 years. You have two children and we still want to complete sentences for you. We make the assumption that you can't do certain things even though you are a wife and mother.

We can't elevate you from the place of being the youngest, the baby of the family but we can respect you for all of your accomplishments as a wife, mother and professional singer. I respect Barbara for following her dream and taking the risk of leaving the security of a job that obviously did not make her happy to pursue her dream to be a professional singer.

I respect her for the courage she displayed in auditioning for Broadway. You have to believe in yourself and in your gift to take these daring steps. I may be older but she has a stronger will and brave spirit.

There are so many dimensions to the person Barbara. In addition to being wife, mother and psalmist, Barbara is a Pastor's wife, the leading lady of a devoted congregation. In this role she shares her husband, her family and time with many people. She is called on to meet the needs of many people. She is a supportive partner in her husband's calling. I know this has not always been an easy role for Barbara, but God continues to develop her in this special place. Many women view this as an enviable role, only because they do not understand the sacrifice and responsibility attached to it. I may be older, but I admire the dignified manner in which Barbara allows the Lord to use her in this appointed place.

I admire many singers, but none more than my sister Barbara. Her music ministry celebrates the gift of song that God has deposited deep inside of her. She ministers to me each time I hear her sing. I may be older but I admire the way Barbara is being used by God to reach His people with her voice.

My sister Barbara is one of my strongest supporters. She believes that I can do anything and respects my accomplishments. She shares her children with me and as such has allowed me to feel unconditional love. When I needed encouragement I have often been surprised by the strength of the love of a child. I may be older but often Barbara displays the wisdom and insight that comes with time and experience. She has the "mother wit" that my mother possessed. She is my friend forever.

Carolyn McLaughlin

Dear_____,

This letter is to my Momma,

I see so many parents who are tired of being in the struggle of daily challenges that exist for single parents. I see parents who have given up because they have no motivation or direction. I see children who enter school with no aspirations for succeeding in school.

Momma, you were a single parent who had to have faced some of the challenges that still exist. The difference is the way in which you handled those challenges. Growing up, my brother and I were taught education is the key to whatever it is you choose to do. The only limits are the ones you place upon yourself. I remember you saying you wanted us to do better than you had done, which meant graduating near the top of our high school class and pursuing our goals one step at a time and never giving up on our dreams.

Growing up we watched you take person after person into our home, who would have otherwise not had a place to go and you are still doing it. Your kindness and generosity taught me that when you are blessed you must pass the blessings on.

You have been an undying source of support in any task that I have taken on. You instilled my sense of work ethic you kept me focused when I tried to deviate from the plan. You provided the discipline needed, when my goals were about to become a reality. The very best thing of all—you did this by yourself and with an unconditional love that still carries me through any obstacles that life has for me. I want to say Thank You.

If there were any advice to give to young single parents who have lost their way, it would be lead by example. When obstacles are placed before you, go over them, around them or through them to model the persistence children need to succeed in life.

Patricia Cox

Dear_____,

I had no idea in my younger childhood that we were poor. We lived in the project of downtown St. Louis, Mo. And my world was always made to appear safe and sound.

My mother who was the oldest of 17 children, worked hard as a single parent, always handling the demands and pressures of raising two children alone, and later in her mid life, a set of twins.

Although my father was visible at times in my life, I grew up in a single-parent household with my mother who shaped the foundation for my moral values, helped me
develop coping skills and gave me the stamina to handle life's disappointments.

My impression of our life growing up was that there was always plenty of food, we always looked presentable and each day was as good as the next. There was silence on a lot of things, for which I later realized was because my mother did not want to expose us to her fears, worries and personal tragedies.

It wasn't until I was much older that I found out the truth about our lives. Many of our meals were bought on credit from the neighborhood Jewish grocer and from day to day my mother had no idea where our next money would come from or how we would live.

My mother was an expert seamstress and sewed most of my clothing. I always longed for store bought clothes and considered mine, "home made." I did not understand why my teachers were so impressed with my clothes or with the fact that I had my own personal tailor. I did not see the love, effort, and the time that she sacrificed so that my self—esteem would not suffer and that our poverty would not reflect itself.

I always believed we walked miles to the free dentist, because the weather was beautiful, not because that dime had to be saved for our next meal. Mother displayed a great amount of resilience, skill and guts as she accepted each challenge, even in what appeared to be no-win situations.

She stressed the importance of my education and demanded college for all of us, because she always stated that her children would not grow up in poverty and suffer the hardships that she endured all of her life. We had no money, yet somehow she made sure that all four of her children were educated, some even earned Masters Degrees.

There are so many ways I conscientiously and unconsciously imitate her. I have yet to have obtained the strength she portrayed.

I do not have wealth, or all the things that I desire, and I have yet to reach my goals in life. Even so, I will forever have in my suitcase the things that she taught me.

She taught me life lessons and strength. I know that I will emerge a stronger woman because of her.

Joyce King

Dear_____,

What a roller coaster ride!

We've been on more roller coaster rides than any theme park with the longest line of people.

Here's how the ride started. She was five. I was twelve—Why do I have to babysit you, I'd rather be with my "almost" teenage girlfriends, giggling and flirting with boys.

But, through the years, things changed and I saw you grow physically, mentally, emotionally and socially. You were this tiny "squirt" that always cried when I ran out of the house without you, now you're my best friend. How did that ever happen? Blood bonded us, love made us best friends.

You're pregnant! Oh my God, I'm having a niece or nephew. And you want me to be your what! Coach, how exciting!!!. Although we were suppose to be serious during Lamaze class we had so many laughs and fun and what a wonderful experience for both of us, especially me since I never had children. What about this experience they call "Labor".

No more laughing and having fun. This is the real thing not a dress rehearsal, we need to be serious. She had a pretty rough road.

It's a boy, but "I" wanted a girl. He's so cute (handsome) and of course, I wouldn't change a thing about him, not even 18 years later.

It's early October 2000 and time for our yearly mammograms. Mine was A-ok, there's a shadow on Gina's, my sister. The doctor wanted a retake and I assured her it was no big deal. But, unfortunately, it was a very big deal. It showed a mass in her left breast.

Now the biopsy, again! I tried to assure her that it would be negative. The next few days of waiting were dreadful each day longer than the day before. How long does this take? What if my sister's mass "whatever" is malignant? How will I deal with this to get her and the family through? I felt my stress level build, knots in my stomach and I don't have a good feeling about this. As each day slowly goes by, I wait for the phone to ring with some kind of news—good or bad—I had to be ready for the ride ahead.

It's a calm day, October 10, 2000. I had no idea what a fury of a day it was going to be. Around 10am, my phone rings, I look at my phone display and her number appears. I sit for only a few seconds before I answer. As I said hello, her voice was trembling. "Jo, its malignant." I couldn't answer her. I was shocked and was trying to hold back my tears.

I told her I'd be over in 10 minutes.

How would I handle this! My sister, her family, our mother—before I got to them I had to calm down because I needed to be strong for them. I never thought I'd make it to her house. As I put the receiver down tears flowed uncontrollably and when I looked up all my friends were around me. How did they know? It only took one of them to see me crying and know in just that split second that our lives had changed.

When I arrived at Gina's I took a deep breath and walked in the door. Our eyes met and I went over to her and we hugged and cried, (this was the beginning of a lot of tears) she was trembling and so was I. Could I tell her again that it would be alright?

Our first visit to the oncologist was frightening. Positive, he said. But, as I sat listening and taping the consultation visit, my gut was telling me the opposite.

It was a very, very, difficult road for Gina, but after 2 years, there's a great ending to this story, she's still here. Now, I don't say "some-day". I thank God for "today" because we might not be here tomorrow.

Our ride is not over by a long shot but for now, we have made it through together, still laughing and fighting and sometimes looking back and saying "What a Ride'!

Jo DeLucia-Berkley

Dear_____,

Each year, as we approach Mother's Day, I am reminded of Mama and what a powerful mother she is. I feel her presence whenever I am called on to do something special or face a new challenge. For all that I am and in all that I achieve, I never fail in some small way to give her credit and honor. People across the nation and indeed in the world know or should know of Miss Willie Mae and the town called Shubuta in Mississippi. And, if they don't know of this remarkable woman's story, "Ill tell it, " as the gospel song says "whenever I go."

When I think of Mama, I picture a parent who loved her children dearly— all 14 of us. As the oldest, I was privy to some of her special qualities. I believe our mother was unique for her times, and she obviously felt the same about us. She thought we could do anything.

She praised and supported us unceasingly. She could rise to just about any occasion. Once pumped up, she consoled and cajoled, pampered and petted, patted, prayed and cried. Like me, she could cry—and I assume I inherited the trait from her—at the drop of a hat. Speaking of which, she wore so many hats.

She was a nurse. She calmed our fears while soothing our fevers, spooning out the castor oil with a twist of lemon. And, don't forget the tallow tea, and the Vicks vapor rub and cod liver oil!

She was a gourmet cook. She put a hurt'n' on a mouth-watering de-lectable—chicken pot- pie or liver and onions. Both dishes were gar-nished with a hefty helping of golden corn bread. But, I don't want to slight the tastiness of her scrumptious dumplings or her duplicate-defying dressing. Both, were Umm Ummph!

She was a poet, playwright and singer, not to mention author, analyst, speechwriter, lecturer, (we all remember those lectures) and dramatizer.

In fact, she could recite Paul Lawrence Dunbar's poetry almost as well as he could. In addition, she was an ace at trigonometry. (If Aunt Zella was alive, she could vouch for that.) In my later years, I learned that this unassuming, renaissance woman whom I was always so privi-leged to call mother was also a dancer, sharing on (rare) occasions her talent for doing "The Charleston."

Most of all, Mama was an earner of respect by all who came in contact with her and many did, especially through her far-reaching involvement in HeadStart and Friends of Headstart.

For example, Dr. Shirley Jones, then Dean of Social Work at the University of Southern Mississippi in Hattiesburg, knew Mama back in the early days of the HeadStart movement. Dr. Jones ran a rural project out of the University that often took her to Mississippi Valley State in Itta Bena. When Mama, who was going to school there, met Dr. Jones, I think my mother made a lifelong impression on Shirley Jones, one the professor will never forget.

Whenever I speak or make presentations, I always mention how my mother influenced my life. I never fail to do so. It is great to have a mother who is so strong of conviction, so committed of faith and so generous of heart. Mama, for all you give, for the beautiful woman you are, we thank you for being a loving presence in our lives. We honor you always.

Anne Pope

Dear_____,

This letter is to my mother who recently passed away. There is no relief for the pain I feel due to your absence. I have so many things to tell you. I need your advice. I crave the comfort of your touch. I long for the peace that comes from knowing that you were always there for me. Even when we disagreed, I knew that you did not find me disagreeable. My only source of comfort lies in the thought of you being at peace, living with the Lord, Daddy, Joanne, Mae Doris and all of those who were there to greet you upon your arrival.

Your "mother wit" served as a crystal ball into all of our lives. As a teenager, I recall you saying to me "I can't be your friend, I'm your mother." I didn't understand at the time but in reality you were my best friend. No matter what problem I had, you always knew what to say to comfort me.

Later as an adult you often said. "You wouldn't be what you are or have what you have if it weren't for me and your daddy." Truer words were never spoken. You often stated that my sister-in laws should be grateful to you for raising such wonderful husbands as my brothers. They work hard and are good providers for their families. The apple didn't fall far from the tree.

There are many principles that you upheld throughout your life that stand out for me.

You were a woman of integrity, a woman of peace. I never knew you to be angry with anybody or to hold a grudge against anyone.

You always told me to pray for my enemies and to be kind to them.

You often stated, "You can catch more bees with honey." I have no memory of you ever being in conflict with anyone. I have no memory of you being one to gossip or being the topic of any gossip. You were an independent woman, with very select, special friends.

I often wondered if you were lonely after Daddy passed away but, I discovered that you were good at entertaining yourself. You were secure in yourself and enjoyed your own company. I am learning the value of solitude. I honor you for your courage and brave spirit.

You never gave up and believed that you deserved the best of everything.

The older I get the more I find myself becoming just like you. As I dress myself each day I see you. Memories of being in your bedroom as a child watching you and helping you get dressed flood my mind.

Visualizing how you selected your stylish hats, matching shoes and purse and flattering suits and dresses, clarifies where I get my appreciation of fine things. I want you to know that I have the white bowl with the gold lines etched through it sitting on my dining room table. I recall your potato salad in that bowl as a child and I will take good care of it.

I revisit your final months and helping you get dressed too. I tried to maintain the pride and dignity you wore so well in selecting your daily attire. It pleased me and consoled me to be able to select clothing for you that you enjoyed wearing. I remember when you would cut patterns from newspaper and make outfits for all of your girls.

I loved wearing clothes that you made for me. I particularly remember an Easter outfit, which consisted of a pink dress with a pink and white cape.

There has never been a more devoted wife and mother than you. The love you demonstrated for your husband and your children is training material for young wives and mothers. We always came first. You denied yourself to make us happy. The creativity you exhibited in meeting our needs was not appreciated at the time but has paid great dividends in each of our lives. Thank you for providing an education for me that you never had. I tried to do things in my life that would honor you. I hope I made and continue to make you proud.

A gentle giant is what you were. Not only did you meet the needs of your household, but you blessed other households as well. You taught us the meaning of sharing, not just amongst ourselves but with anyone that is in need. Nobody knows all of the times you reached out to help someone in need.

I am the beneficiary of your investment in our community. I realize now that I was destined to become a member of the Albany, New York Common Council when you and Daddy became entrepreneurs in McLaughlin's Grocery, in the South End of Albany. I wouldn't be who and what I am if it were not for you.

I never heard you utter the words "I wish I had" done this or that. This leads me to believe that you had a complete life. Even though I miss you terribly, I believe that you fulfilled all of your dreams.

Whatever your heart desired to do, I believe you followed through and made it happen. You understood that God alone had control over you and the circumstances of your life. You knew that "if God be for you, He is more than the whole world against you. I thank God for your bingo excursions and travels to Hawaii. Knowing how happy those annual vacations made you puts a smile on my face. If you could travel by yourself, so can I.

When I sat down to write you this letter, I didn't realize it would have the effect that it has had on me. I have cried, laughed, smiled, meditated, and realized that I cannot express all that I want to say to you in one letter. I will continue to write to you. I take your life experience and keep it in my pocket for a rainy day. It is as valuable as money in the bank.

I just want you to know that I thank you, thank you for being the best friend I could ever have. I rise up to call you blessed. The Bible instructs us to honor our Father and Mother that our days may be long upon this earth. I tried to be obedient to God's word. I hope you knew how much I loved you. I miss you Mama. Please stay close.

Carolyn McLaughlin

Chapter Reflections

Introduction to Chapter 10

DEAR_____,

Some of the first lessons we learned came from our mothers, aunts, and grandmothers. The backdrop was the kitchen where we saw them slice, dice, cut up, stir, pound and pour those ingredients together to create those delicious Sunday meals, Christmas dinners and Thanksgiving feasts.

But we saw these women we love do more than teach us how to feed our bodies. From them we leaned how to sustain our souls. They taught us how to be ladies. They taught us how to persevere, how to step up to the line and then step over it.

They were women of character.

This chapter celebrates and thanks those women, as well as the women we did not grow up with but noticed from afar for all the lessons learned. They are women with principles, women who earned Masters Degrees in determination and PhD's in fearlessness. We thank them for all that they sacrificed for us. They have blessed us and taught us lessons we could never have learned from a book!

Elaine

Philippians 4- 9

... Whatever you have learned or received or heard from me or seen in me, put it into practice.

Women As Blessings, The Lessons They Teach Us

Dear_____,

Shelly is a beautiful women with big brown eyes, a flawless complexion and a hearty laugh. She's the kind of person that whenever you are with her you can't help but have a good time. Her smile is infectious. (I'm smiling now just thinking about her.)

But it's not just what you see outwardly that makes Shelly the kind of person you want to hang out with, its what's inside too. She's a woman of great character and courage. In fact, she is one of the strongest women I know. She has that "I'm not giving up, I don't care what comes or what goes," kind of strength. When she tells you about some of the things she's had to overcome it makes you want to stop whining and buck up. She just makes you want to be a better person.

To what do I attribute her courage? I don't know, perhaps it's the fact that she is the mother of eight kids. Surely, raising all those beautiful, intelligent human beings, who I believe will do great things for this world, has helped her remain strong. But, I'm a firm believer that we are all born with strengths that whenever we need them emerge and help us to persevere. So, that means like a new car, some of Shelly's traits are "standard."

I thank God that our paths crossed because like her smile, her courage has rubbed off on me too. A while back she taught me a very important lesson about friendship and about courage.

I was going through a very painful and difficult time and she knew about it.

One day after work I returned home to find this message on my answering machine.

BEEP! Hi, Elaine this is Shelly. I called you at work figured you were there. The Lord laid you on my heart and I just wanted to call and have a word of prayer. Just wanting you to know like I know you already know, that God is more than able.

He's bigger than our circumstances. He's greater than our struggles. And, I just called to encourage you great woman of God to hold your head up! And, you know what, through every battle it is God. Even though we think we're in the midst of it, God is fighting our battles.

And, we just have to stand still and wait for Him to bring about a change. I thank Him through every storm "we change". Not only does the storm seem to rise, the billows blow, but "we also change." God is building character and integrity in the people of God. So, on this day God we thank you for our sister.

Thank you for being the God of peace. Thank you for being the God of all comfort. Thank you for being the God of understanding. Thank you for being our banner Lord and on today we just lift up Elaine BEEP!

When I got home and heard the message, I was so encouraged I had to play it again. I played it a third time and then I started yelling, YEAH, YEAH, YEAH, when she said "Great woman of God, and God is bigger than our circumstances. He's bigger than our struggles."

Then I started to cry. How blessed I was to have a friend who would pray for me such a special, personal prayer. It was a great lesson in courage and friendship.

Elaine Houston

Dear_____,

If you look up the word "GUTSY" in the dictionary you may not find it. But, my personal definition would be strong, courageous, intestinal fortitude, determined. Right next to all those words would be a picture of my mother Lizzie Leah Fox.

One of my most vivid memories of her "moxie" was when I was 13 or so. We, my mother, brothers, sister and I lived in a housing project. Although, I was just barely a teenager, I was tall and I caught the eye of a kid living in the building behind me. He too was tall for his age. About six two, 16 or 17 and very lanky. Sadly for him he was just not to my liking. But, he wouldn't take no for an answer and persisted in his quest for me to be his girl. Finally, he got it but he didn't like my answer and in response told me he was going to beat me up! (Love will make you do strange things!!!!!!)

So he waited for me after school but I managed to ditch him. But, I was scared of him and soon my mother found out about it. Huh, Oh! She marched me right over to his house and bravely knocked on the door. When his mom answered, she yelled, "Tell your son to come here, he wants to hit my child." The boy heard all the commotion and came to the door and my mom lit into him! She told him if he touched me she had something for his blank, blank, blank! All the while she was yelling at him she was motioning to her coat pocket.

Well, not to be out done, he was yelling back that he was going to get me after school. That's when she told him "Hit her now, hit her now." I was scared to death and praying that he wouldn't take her up. But, the two of them just kept at it. Finally, he got it and we walked away, with my mother still calling him everything in the book, but a child of God! As we walked home I realized that my mother wasn't just pretending. She had a gun in her pocket! She was going to shoot him! This little fireball had a gun in her pocket and was threatening bodily harm! Thank God he didn't hit me.

It was from this lesson that I learned how men are supposed to treat women and I never dated a guy that beat me up. I wasn't having any of that!

I can recall numerous times my mother went to bat for us, like a lioness protecting her cubs she stood up to people who treated us unfairly and always encouraged us to stand up for ourselves.

One of those times, she had to protect us from a very cruel stranger. My mom worked nights in a factory.

On her way to work she was mugged. This coward hit her over the head and stole her purse.

In her purse were the keys to the house and the mailbox. The next day the mugger left a note in the mailbox demanding money or he would kill us. I guess my mom had pictures of us in her wallet. It was a very scary and sad time. No child likes to think of their parent being hurt and then have to worry about their safety too.

I remember my mother sitting us down and telling us what had happen. She told us we would have to be careful and that we now had to start coming home from school together and hold hands.   Nothing ever happened and my mother never let on to us that she was scared and the night after this happened to her she went back to work. Never missing a beat. She is really a brave woman. Now that I'm an adult, I try to do everything I can to make my mom's life better and comfortable. Three years ago, I started taking her on vacations. We've gone to Paris, France, and London, England. Right now, we are gearing up for a trip to Florence, Italy. I remember on our trip to Paris, the two of us sat in the garden at the estate of the famous sculptor, Rodin. We were talking about how far we had come since those days in the housing projects. And, what I know without a doubt is that I would be nothing if it were not for my mom. She's taught me so many great lessons. Thanks mom.

Elaine Houston

Dear_____,

If you are looking for an expression of God you will find it when you look at me. If you are pondering this statement, believe me, I had to ponder it myself before I knew who I was and what my purpose was in life. I was 47-years-old before I knew who I really was.

I had gone through failures, anger, fear, doubt, opposition, broken promises, isolation, depression, judgment, and yes there were some victories and for years I thought I was doing a great job at managing my life.

For years I was convinced that I was the one orchestrating my life. I was a master at juggling hats. I was a wife, full time mom, full time college student, and community volunteer.

Yet, what I did not know was that it was God who was in control of things. He was my helper, my counselor, surely He was the one in control.

Even through the separation from my alcoholic husband, which was my first traumatic experience with broken promises, I still thought I was in control. I thought I had to be tough if I was to successfully carry out the two roles of mother and "now" father.

My second traumatic experience was to sit across the table visiting my two precious sons in a dingy, deplorable looking jail cell. As I looked at my sons my body and mind were riddled with guilt, panic, failure, and anger. It was surreal, and I entertained the thought of dying in hopes of awakening and finding out it was only a dream.

But, it wasn't a dream. However, I still thought I was in charge. Prior to my sons' incarceration, in that same jail, I had facilitated life skills groups for female inmates and provided consultations for them. So, I knew judges and lawyers and people in the judicial system. Surely, with the number of hats I was wearing it would be a cinch to get my sons out of jail. I thought I was in charge and that I could get my family out of this nightmare.

Plus, I had the finances. But, this time, God showed me that I was not in charge and that my sons would have to do some time. My youngest was incarcerated for several months. My oldest served four years of a six-year sentence.

It was about that time that I became more willing to hear and listen to the Lord.

In fact, looking back, I know the Lord was trying to get my attention, even though I thought I was the one doing all the reaching out. At the end of every visit with my sons, I ran through the jail parking lot to my car. I was looking for safety, privacy, and a place of refuge to cry out to God. "Help me, Jesus, I screamed." "Help my sons, I yelled."

But, in reality, He was the one reaching out and running towards me. Finally, I reached out and took His hand. It was at this time that I made a phone call to my grandmother. The conversation went like this. " Hello Nana, I called to tell you that I accepted the Lord, I said." I went on to apologize to her for something that I said to her years ago. "Nana, I asked you why you prayed so much. I really did not understand that you were praying for me, I said." My Nana has passed away but she lived to see me accept the Lord. And, I know now that despite the many hats I wore, I was never in charge. God was and He was with me all the time.

Jean Dobbs

Dear_____,

This letter is to my Aunt Missie. I am taking this time to pen this letter, because I haven't told you lately how much your love and affection has always meant to me.

I remember vividly when you were alive and I was growing up in Shubuta, Mississippi, that I would get a missive and could always tell it was from you just by the handwriting. It would be so exciting to open and read it. Your letter was bound to make me happy, because it was filled unfailingly with good news. You never wrote about sad things, only happy things. And, if in my response to you I shared a problem, or like any kid, sounded sad or wanted something, you invariably addressed that in your letter.

You would tell me about new medicines that could help me with ailments, like my asthma. I vividly remember the time you sent me a magazine ad for "Dr. Blosser's Cigarettes" for asthma.

My mother was overjoyed and went out and bought some, so that when I started wheezing from an asthma attack, I would smoke one and often find relief.

You were always concerned about me. You always had a remedy of some kind, something to make things better.

You made me feel that I was your favorite grandniece. You would send me packages of clothes and other goodies and I would feel like a little princess. Then you put me in charge of distributing what I didn't want to my cousins. That, of course, made me feel as if I was "all that," as they say, "and a bag of chips." You had confidence in me and you helped me develop confidence in myself, and, boy do I have self-confidence. Thank you,
Aunt Missie.

I remember, vividly, wanting to come to Philadelphia to live with you and you told me how much violence there was in Philly. Well, you would be surprised if you were alive
today. You could never have imagined, not in a million years, how bad it would become. Thanks again.

But, I loved to come down and visit you and uncle Earl. You were so kind and generous. You spoiled me even as an adult. I loved your spaghetti and meatballs. You were the only cook I know who put cheese in the sauce. Creamy........ummm! Not to mention your turkey dressing with turkey tails. Rich.....ummm!

I can see you now, sitting on the day bed in the living room, looking out the window "controlling" (surveying) 28th Street. You had earned the love and respect of the people in the neighborhood, and even though the neighborhood had changed, becoming somewhat violent and unsafe, no one dared bother you. You were a GEM.

I think often of how the fish man came with fresh fish, the fruit man came with fresh fruit, blueberries and other fresh berries, and the vegetable man came with fresh vegetables. They all came and made a special presentation to "Miss Walker"— Mother Walker.

You gained the respect of the clergy, townspeople, elected officials, church folk and all who came in contact with you. You didn't take no stuff! You were a role model for all women, especially young woman, and most especially for me. God bless you.

Anne Pope

Dear_____

This letter is to my sixth grade teacher. Your inspiration has been a catalyst for my career in education. You had insight into the difficulties I was experiencing during my time in sixth grade. The onset of puberty took me on an emotional roller coaster. I did not have the knowledge or the experience to know what I needed or how to go about getting it.

When I entered your classroom, you instantaneously tapped into my emotions. You invited me into your home to meet your family. You took me to special events as if I were a part of your family. You were constantly challenging me to meet and exceed your expectations in class. You gave me the push I needed to maximize my potential. In doing so, you and I connected emotionally because I knew you had my best interest at heart and research now shows that African American children learn better when they are connected emotionally.

I also remember my first class as a teacher, which was a challenge that I wasn't sure I could meet. I came to see you to cry on your shoulders and expected a soft place to land, but you would have none of that. Instead, you gave me a harsh send off with "I know you can handle it." At the time I thought it was cold and harsh, but it gave me the push I needed, to gather strength for picking my battles and winning the fight for education. By the way, that incident gave me a lot of what still motivates me nineteen years later.

My goal is to impress upon new teachers an understanding that, "If you're in it for the money, you won't last. If you're in it for the accolades, that will pass. If you're in it to guide students away from their challenges towards a bright future, TIME IS WINDING DOWN—FAST.

Patricia Cox

Dear_____,

Many of us have fond memories of our grandmother. We remember her unconditional love and also her wisdom and understanding.

My "Gram" was such a woman.

At the age of 25 she married and she and her husband raised four sons, including a set of identical twins, and one daughter. They worked together and loved each other, not only meeting life's challenges. But, overcoming great difficulties.

Their second child was still born at full term. They weathered the Great Depression and lived with her mother to help out the family, even though her husband had lost his job. He was without steady work for over two years, yet each day he went out to look for work, any work he could find to support his family. The family wasn't even aware he had lost his job.

During WWII all four sons were in military action. My father, who was shot down in a glider, was a P.O.W. for almost a year. Another son was gravely wounded during the Battle of the Bulge.

To show you how her children were raised, my father who was mistreated as a P.O.W. became the military Governor for an area in Germany after his liberation and recovery. Instead of revenge for how he was treated, he governed with justice and kindness. Later he was elected by the town as Mayor, the first American to ever receive this honor.

As a youngster growing up, to me "Gram" was the kindest, most patient and loving person I had ever known. She never raised her voice she didn't have to raise it. I always wanted to be good and do well for her. The thought of doing wrong never came to mind, she was so good.

This wonderful woman taught me how to live. She exemplified what was taught to me as a child by all the teachers and family. She had strong faith in God and great love for her husband and family. Always, she put their needs before hers and she realized the joys of peace and grace. "Gram" also taught not to gossip. Her advice was that before you say anything about someone, ask yourself:

1. Is what I am going to say true?
2. It is necessary?
3. Will it hurt someone?

After "Gram' died in 1974 a folded up note, which she had written, was found in her address book. It was titled "For Happy Family Living" The nine points express some of her convictions for raising children. What she wrote follows....

For Happy Family Living

Written by Islay Macdonald Prentice

1. Say what you feel and don't try to put on an act in front of either your partner or your children.

2. Make your children masters of their own fate just as fast as they can accept responsibilities, so they will grow swiftly into independence and self-reliance.

3. Learn to live with your differences—be willing to give and take for the common good.

4. Make sure all your children know you "love them like the dickens" and that in any emergency you will drop everything and stand right by them.

5. Enjoy the extra special fun that can come only from doing things together as a family.

6. Encourage each child to develop along his own natural lines and glory in the fact that he may turn out altogether different from you.

7. Train each child to think in terms of how his actions look to others. That way he will be less self-centered and get into less trouble.

8. Help your children to be good losers as well as good winners.

9. Show your children the excitement and satisfaction that comes from trying to discover new ways to make this world a pleasanter place to live. That is creative living.

The love and lessons "Gram" gave me are still with me today—and now I am a Grandmother. With God's help, I hope to be able to share at least some of the lessons and love she gave. I pray that each of you will be able to share the love so freely given by God with those around you.

Caroline P. Gomez

Dear_____,

You thought your husband was your best friend too, and now you have doubts. Let me tell you honey why this type of relationship may be the hardest of all, but also the most rewarding.

A lot of women ask me the secret to my relationship with my husband. I tell them there isn't one! But, here are some tips in italics. After 34 years with the same man I have learned a few things.

First of all a love relationship, a real romantic friendship needs to be built on mutual trust, understanding, shared vision, truth, honesty, similar values, humor and respect. You know how some people actually grow to look alike, not us. We are both so different.

Look at why you married him. Sometimes it actually helps to *make a list* and keep it handy for a quick reference. Honest I did this once, and it was a great reminder when I wanted to wring his neck. It helps to remember why you fell in love. Now, write, before you forget.

Then remember to be forgiving. *Always forgive him.* It's like cleaning out an old junk drawer. You know its there. But no one else needs to know, only you two. *Keep your relationship sacred.*

Okay, so you have crying kids, a nasty boss, deadlines, money problems, and you're so tired. Oh, how well I remember those days, and who would come home and take a nap?

Not you, I know. A man can usually sleep in spite of what is happening at the moment. It doesn't make it better. Look at your list. *But, make a date with him, a real date, for just the two of you. Keep this time special.* Did you know the cheapest meal to eat out is usually breakfast, and babysitters aren't so hard to find later on a Saturday or Sunday morning. Try a breakfast date once a week. Don't break it for anyone. We started this years ago, and now we do it because we still like it and each other.

Does this best friend relationship sound like work? It does and it is. But, hang in there. *You both can't get angry at the same time. Timing is everything.* Above all never seek revenge. God has a way of dealing with those that need it. God can be so creative. *Let him handle your husband. Pray for him. It's hard to pray for someone and remain angry.* I've had those times when I actually ripped a cupboard door off its hinges. I also know this same man that could make me so darn angry was the same one that brought me home a string bikini as a gift, after I had three children. I laughed, and I never did wear it. I still have it put away. But he was so honest in how he felt about me.

I can tell you horror stories about how he refused to ask for directions. How awful it was to be away from him when he traveled for work and how stressful money problems used to be. How we could both get so upset at each other at the worst possible times. He can still tick me off better than anyone I know.

This is also the same guy that cried when I received my Bachelor's degree, after years of putting it off. Waited with me helplessly, as we heard yet more bad news about people we love, went through chemo with me and surprised me with a hot tub for my birthday. He also built a stone wall on the hottest July day because he knew I wanted one. Is the romance still alive and well? You decide. Last night, we went on a romantic sleigh ride for two in Vermont. It was twelve degrees outside. We didn't even feel the cold.

With much encouragement,

Linda S. Bruno

Dear_____,

This story begins with a young woman who loved to dream. She began with a dream of being a fancy director of a line of cruise ships. She would often dream of the day she would set sail on the sea with thousands of other people on board. She would gather any and all literature on cruise ships.

Slowly she began to put together all pieces of what she needed to do to accomplish her dream to make it a reality. School was coming to a close and the young lady would soon be graduating from high school. Then, she would move on to the school where she would receive specialize training in the career she would soon enter.

On this particular day, the young woman is having lunch at a restaurant with some of her friends. As she is saying her goodbyes to them a young gentleman approaches her. After formal introductions are made a lengthy conversation takes place with her new acquaintance.

They exchange phone numbers and addresses and she says goodbye. As time goes on, they grow closer and closer but each must depart for their own journey in life. While away, they write and call each other as much as possible. The young man began to get restless and is tired of the long distance relationship. He then decided to ask her to marry him. She agreed, knowing that she had not yet completed her course of study. As time passes, they married and start a family. And, now here she is with a young child, newly married and entering into a new journey in her life called motherhood.

She still holds very dear in her heart the dream she once had.

As time goes on she finds the time to finish the education she once began. She has a ray of hope and she clings to her faith that one day she will go on to complete her life long dream. But first, she is enjoying the stage of life she is in called, Motherhood.

Tonjia Newman

Dear_____,

For virtually all my life, I have sustained a deep and abiding faith in God. It is a faith that was nurtured early on by a loving and talented mother, of whom I harbor the fondest memories. This letter is a tribute to my mother Willie Mae and another powerful and influential woman in my life, my aunt Annie Mae. Whatever I am or whatever I will be, I owe to the teachings and training of these two women and of course God's word. It has taught me that with Him everything is possible. The efforts of my mother and aunt served to reinforce His word. Their teachings have shaped my life.

I am the oldest of fourteen children. Needless to say that within a family that large, there is a great deal of diversity. There is the older set of siblings. The oldest were the guinea pigs for what would later become a model for raising children. While growing up, the oldest were not allowed to play cards, for example, although it became all right for the youngsters. When I asked my mother why the difference, why was it that they could do things forbidden us, she replied simply and honestly, "I don't know, I guess I learned from the older children that it was all right."

My mother taught us by example, by maxims, by lectures, by what-ever means she felt were necessary to raise strong children. She suc-ceeded in that all twelve of us, who lived through childhood, two died as infants, have some formal education. God has blessed all of us to be alive and self sustaining. We now take care of her in her illness.

Willie Mae was bright, articulate, fashionable and beautiful. She loved her children to a fault. She thought we were talented enough to do anything. She told us we could do all things through Christ who strength-ens us. Through sayings, she gave us a creed that beneficially shaped our habits, "If a task is once begun, never leave it till it's done."
"Be the labor great or small, do it well or not at all." She taught us to do things right the first time, under penalty of having to do them a second time. "You've got to lick that calf again, " she would say if we did a task halfheartedly.

Willie Mae's teachings have accompanied me through life. I respect and believe in her because I saw what she produced. I witnessed the fruits of her labors.

She was a writer, poet, orator, philosopher, teacher, dramatist, and even a preacher, at least to us children when we did something wrong.

Above all, she was a storyteller, regaling us with real-life stories that helped shape our lives.

In the town we grew up in, a small mid eastern Mississippi community called Shubuta, Mama taught us how to cope with our circumstance, whether segregated or integrated. Whatever the situation, our mother supported us both physically and morally. She always made the times relevant by telling us true stories that would paint a picture of what it was like to live during the "dark days" of segregation in the South.

In one instance, a Mrs. V. was walking along a sidewalk in downtown, the segregated Shubuta and failed to move aside for a white woman.

Her husband slapped Mrs. V., causing the hapless Negro woman to urinate on herself.

In another instance, she told us about the time three Negro boys were murdered by some of the white townsmen for allegedly whistling at a white girl while they were passing beneath a bridge.

The men took the boys out of town to the hanging bridge, lynched them and had their bodies brought back for their parents to bury their brutally murdered sons. My mother did not spare the gruesome details, she even told us their names, so that we might understand what we faced when we had to interact with whites.

You see, my mother had experienced racism first-hand. On at least one occasion, her father, a sharecropper, confronted racism head-on.

As she related it, my mother and her siblings would play with the children of the white sharecroppers.

Like most youngsters, they had their scrapes and fights. Once or perhaps more than once, Papa Zean's kids whipped their white playmate's behinds and they ran home and told their own fathers. That night after dark, the white men, wearing Ku Klux Klan robes and bearing shotguns, rode out to my grandfather's house. He put out the lights and sat by the door awaiting their arrival. When they did they were greeted by a barrage of less than friendly shotgun fire. The episode won him the respect of the townsmen.

So my mother grew up with a father who earned himself a full measure of civic respect. He was a pillar of the community, as indeed, she was destined to become. Blacks and whites from all walks of life respected her and it was from her that I learned the importance of living an upright life. Dignity and respect have always been important to me. I work hard to maintain that and honor. I make it a point to let my word be my bond. I have my mother to thank for that.

I am proud to be Miss Willie Mae's daughter.

Anne Pope

Dear_____,

Sometimes God works in the most unexpected ways. My friend Cynthia came as an unexpected gift in my life. She has shown me a glimpse of living a graceful life, of not being fettered about everyday situations that could easily turn into drama.

I met Cynthia when I lived in Albany, NY. I had moved to that area for a way out of a job I hated and to be near a boy I felt I would marry. He actually asked me to marry him before I moved there. As the Lord would have it, our relationship was not to be and we broke up and my heart broke. It felt as though my heart had broken so many times.

While alone, I started working on a book I had an idea about some time ago. I needed an artist to illustrate the drawings I had in my head but didn't have the talent to transfer to paper. I went to the Kinko's in Colonie, New York looking for help and the girl working there said I should talk to a lady who came in looking for an illustrator for her book. I took the lady's work number and called her. She was a Rensselaer County, New York legislator. Her name was Cynthia Engel. I left a message for her to call me back and she did.

When I explained my reason for calling, about my book. She started to cry on the phone. She apologized and said it was the first time she had cried since her house had burned down. She said the book idea reminded her of something her grandfather had given her that burned in the house fire. She explained that her home burned to the ground while she attended a campaign fundraiser. After some questioning I figured out that I had reported on that fire.

At the time, I was a news reporter at the NBC affiliate in Albany.

Although she and I had never met, she lived only a few miles from me. I saw her picture everyday on a billboard a mile from my home. She wanted us to meet in person for lunch. So, a few days later, we did.

While at lunch, I cried my eyes out. I had just had a broken engage-ment and I could barely function. Cynthia was such a comfort to me. She consoled me. She listened. She accepted me. Despite my emo-tional state, we had a nice visit and we became buddies. We started going to church together. And, not just one church different churches every week. I met her family, her husband, Kevin, their two daugh-ters, Courtney and Angela and son Justin. This was a woman with a full life, tons of friends, a political position and time for me. I was closer to her daughter's age than hers. Still, we enjoyed each other's company.

We talked a lot, about the Lord, life and love. We laughed. We cried. We laughed til we cried. I met her parents. We all spent a lovely December day together in New York City. We ate at the Plaza Hotel.

The lunch buffet there cost $55.00. I remember I saved the receipt to show my dad the bill. That night in the hotel room we all shared, as I lay in the bed, I counted the 22 different items I ate on the buffet. We laughed so much about that. We had come home early that evening after seeing Les Miserable, my first Broadway show. Cynthia didn't feel good.

I remember in her quiet way she told me in a matter of fact way I needed to talk to someone about my mother's death. My mom died when I was a child. As one of 6 kids, there wasn't much time or know-how to deal with grieving children. Cynthia was right but I never got around to it.

Sometime later, we found out why Cynthia didn't feel good in New York. She had a brain tumor. She never said the word cancer, but after several operations, she didn't need to. Even at the hospital, she tried to find me a husband. After her first chemotherapy session, I treated her to a Friendly's sundae in a cup at the hospital cafeteria called "Choices." While there talking to Cynthia about her children and about being the child of a mom who didn't get to finish the job of raising her kids, I cried, again.

The tears pouring down my face didn't keep an attractive man from coming up to us to say he watched me on television. It was surreal. I thanked him but told him my friend and I was having a "moment." She made me go after him to thank him, again. She wanted to see if he was single. He wasn't.

Cynthia was sick but she kept living her life. She enjoyed life. Our birthdays were just weeks apart. She wore a wig after the chemo. So, on our birthday dinner, we both wore wigs out. It was a great night Cynthia, Kevin and Cynthia's parents—Too fun.

Every time I came to see Cynthia, I would bring her a Dunkin' Donuts coffee. It was the same when I got the call that she didn't have long to live. After getting a flat tire fixed, I stopped to get her a new Chai coffee from Dunkin' Donuts that I knew she had to try. By the time I got to her home with it, she couldn't drink. She knew I was there. She held my hand and as the Lord would have it, I was there when she drew her last breath. I had to go tell her beloved sister and Kevin. As I look back, it was a privilege to be with her when she met the Lord. It was a gift. Cynthia wanted me to get help in dealing with my mother dying at such a young age, hers and mine. The help came from seeing my friend die to this world and go on to the next. It came from being able to talk to her children about losing a mother.

Cynthia continues to be with me. I miss her and I love her. I wouldn't ask her to come back here. She knew where she was going.

Know the Lord. Live life. Enjoy it with friends.

Karen Lehane

Dear_____

Of all the matriarchs I've ever seen, she was the pinnacle. Orphaned at a very young age, along with my maternal grandmother, Aunt Louesa Porcher Gilliard Rose Gadsden did her very best, sacrificing, educating, training and caring for those who were abandoned and neglected until the end.

I was bewildered by her death. A woman who had done so much for her family, died alone. Perhaps it was meant to be that way. She always told me. "You were born alone, weren't you? Don't be afraid to do things alone or to live alone." She had only one biological daughter, but countless others passed through her home and received her know how.

She often said to me, "You can't necessarily take your family with you everywhere you go. God has some things for you and only you to do and you must do them alone with His strength." I never understood those words when I was young, but now I SEE and understand.

In the end, Aunt Louesa and my maternal grandmother, Binah, were the only two survivors of seven children. A brother lived a long life and died, but they were never close.

There are things in a person's character that you only discern after they have long departed. I remember being seven years old when my aunt Louesa sat me down to a sewing machine and started teaching me to sew. "You need to help your mother with your brothers and sister, she'd always say". It was prophetic. Somehow I think she knew our father would die. She always seemed to have time for family and knew how to make and keep a dollar. She always seemed to know more than life in America would ever let her use at that time. We knew how extremely intelligent some of those old people were.

The anger I feel at times, of a system that refuses to accept or acknowledge the normal intelligence of all peoples and give them a chance to express it, runs deep. If only they had the chance for education, America would indeed be a better place today.

They never openly expressed hatred of those who hated them or disappointment at their losses, but they pushed us to achieve because of the lives that had been lost in order to provide us with opportunities. But, often you could see it in their faces and countenance.

The summer after my father died, aunt Louesa kept all five of us in South Carolina so my mother could stabilize and finish high school. We really needed that stability and my mother had the opportunity few others ever got with my aunt. I remember how I learned the term "ground nuts". My aunt sent us out into the fields to look for peanuts, which of course, we never found. Then, to our amazement, she pulls the peanuts out of the ground, laughs and tells us about groundnuts. What a shocker!

We learned the importance of the soil and I listened intently to her instructions about how necessary it was to always KNOW HOW to scratch the ground and get food. We learned about priming the pump, washing clothes with a scrub board, taking baths in a tin tub, walking miles to the post office and going to church.

She was a TOUGH, no nonsense person. Life made her that way. She had several failed marriages because the men always liked pretty women, and the women in my family have that typical "Sierra Leone" look. These women always knew where they came from and were very proud that they never lost sight of their culture, like wrapping ones hair with thread.

All of these "little" things are reflected in the personality and persona that I have developed. Without choosing it or knowing the path, I'm more like aunt Louesa than any other female in the family. God has taken all that she taught me to help serve others. And, everything she taught me has been useful in my life as a Christian, wife, mother, teacher, computer programmer and missionary. I'm not at all squeamish about not having running water or having to use an outhouse. Used those in South Carolina, Africa and India. Thank you!

Yes, Aunt Louesa, I did go to the places that God alone selected for me. Me, an Afro-Cuban American woman! I went to India to preach and teach the Gospel with All the credentials that you and God provided. I was the first in that part of India. To my surprise, I found Africans there; people who look just like us. And, I wasn't ashamed of who I was, but I carried what I learned about respect, assimilation and purpose.

Thank you Aunt Louesa for surviving and passing your wisdom on. I'm passing on the little I've been privileged to learn and sharing the opportunities that God has given. I'm also using the examples that you set with your life. Well done, Aunt Louesa. You were faithful with the little you had. And, yes, I went on alone but not without your spirit and God's protective hand. I love you and miss you deeply but will see you again.

Your grandniece,

Loniece

Dear_____,

This letter is for the "New" Career woman. What an exciting time it is to be starting your career. You have a blank canvas upon which to create yourself as a businesswoman. I thought that it might be helpful to you to share with you some of the things that I have learned along the way.

First of all, try to be happy and enjoy what you do. Not everything will go your way and there will be times that nothing seems to be going right, but try to focus on the positive. It will help you feel better and make you more pleasant to be around.

Second, maintain you integrity. A lapse in integrity is virtually impossible to recover from. Do not put yourself in a position where integrity is not respected.

Third, develop expertise and knowledge. You need to "know your stuff" in order to really be a contributor. Do not assume that you do not need to keep learning. Things constantly change and so you need to constantly be developing new expertise and skills.

Fourth, seek change and challenges. Staying in your comfort zone is easy for the short-term, but dull in the long-term. Taking the difficult road does require more effort, but will pay dividends in the end.

Fifth, be kind to others. The business world can be difficult, so try to add some kindness along the way. You will meet some who are so sweet to you if you are important or can do something for them. This is false kindness. Strive to be kind to all— regardless of whether you will get something in return. After all, your kind word to the person cleaning your office may mean more than anything you could ever say to the President of the United States.

Sixth, create a life outside of work. Work will inevitably disappoint you someday and it will be more difficult to deal with this if all you have is work. You will need to make sacrifices for work and it will be all consuming at times. However, carve out time and energy for family, friends and other interests.

Seventh, listen to yourself. You are the best judge of what is right for you.

Eighth, be willing to change course. It is okay to have a goal or destination for your career, but you must be open to unplanned opportunities. If you want to accomplish something big, break it down into small steps.

I hope that this is helpful information for you. Good luck with your career. I'll see you in the Boardroom!

Sincerely,

Victoria M. Stanton

Dear_____,

If I were writing this letter to someone specifically, I'd address it to the woman of the future.

How does it feel to be 95? In a sense, I expected to live a long time because my mother lived to be 91. My father died of a broken neck in an accident in 1925. Back then they didn't have the experience with that type of accident. They did an autopsy and found that his body was in such a condition that he could have lived to be over 100 years old. To live to that age was very unusual for that time period.

How did I get through the tough times? One summer, when I was in my 30's, I worked with a group of refugees from World War II in a synagogue on Amsterdam Avenue and 91st street in New York City. It was so interesting to see these mothers and children from all these foreign countries come as refugees to New York City. For example, there was a French woman and her little boy whom we couldn't understand because we couldn't follow the French. During lunchtime, this little four year old used to get so excited and say "ice cream, ice cream" out loud to us. When he would say these American words, his face would light up. To me, that was a great experience, seeing the excitement in a child who had had nothing but misery.

There were also two, twelve year old boys who had walked all the way from Belgium to Portugal by themselves and lived on what they could pick up from the people who took pity on them. You can't imagine the upheaval that was taking place in Europe at that time.

I felt I wanted to help everyone, because these poor mothers and their children were depending on what we could do for them. I can remember one little 11-yearold boy who was being shown how to play baseball. He got hit in the head by accident and I had to take him to a clinic in New York City on 14th Street on the trolley. We sat in the corridor of this building waiting for help and they came and took him into the examining room. Seeing all the equipment and all that they had to do to help the refugees in the hospital made me feel faint, and I had to go back and sit in the corridor. We did a lot with the children and mothers, teaching them American games such as baseball and cat and mouse, and doing all sort of arts and crafts projects. We even painted scenery for plays that we performed. Our goal was to teach them to speak the English language.

I did these sort of community service projects because it would have been what my father had wanted me to do. He was such an interesting man. His parents were caretakers of a huge estate and it was customary for young men to travel after they finished their early education. Consequently, he learned seven languages while he spent two years traveling. He would get a certificate for going to a new town and report to the police who would provide lodging. He would stay in that town until he learned the language of the territory.

He was able to go to Germany, France, Spain, Italy, Belgium, and England, so he learned German, French, Italian, Spanish and Dutch. He was in charge of setting up the silk mills in Switzerland and was then asked to set up the silk mills in Whitehall, New York. He was well known for supervising the manufacturing of these silk mills.

As I said, he taught me that the best way to learn is by experiencing life first hand. For example, during my visits with my older sister in Montana on the ranch that her husband owned, I was taught how to handle snakes. One of the cowhands showed me how to handle a rattler by holding his head. I also learned how to ride the pinto horses western style.

My parents also took me to Yellowstone National Park when I was eleven. We had a two bedroom cabin with a big woodstove right in the middle. We also cooked food right at the campsite. We fished for trout over in the lake and would cook it almost instantly in the hot springs nearby. Every morning a woodchuck would be sunning on our front step and sleeping under that same step. We fed these animals because they were so tame. One of the things I used to enjoy doing was getting hot water for my father's stove from the Old Faithful geyser, because at that time, all the men used mugs and brushes for shaving.

With my father's parenting philosophy, there was no question that my older sister would be going to college. She was born in 1896 and attended Pratt School of Design in New York. She became an art supervisor for the Schenectady, New York school system.

As for me, I always had a thirst for knowledge which my father encouraged and motivated in me. My mother encouraged me in her own way as well. She used to live on a mountain in Switzerland, and she would travel everyday to learn the tailoring trade.

She tailored my father's wedding suit. He used to be quite a fashion plate, as he sported his wife's work in his white linen suit and panama straw hat. My mother wanted me to branch out as much as I could, but not to the extent that I would be different from other children. My two older sisters and brother also were involved in encouraging my development.

I received a B.A. in Education from Buffalo State College. My first teaching job was teaching first grade in Greenwich Elementary School in New York. I taught for four years in a classroom of 34 children. Then, I was offered the position of teaching in an experimental elementary school in Loudonville, New York.

While I was working as a teacher in Loudonville, I would continue my education traveling to different places, mainly New York City in order to get my Master's Degree in Advanced education. I was hoping to obtain my PhD and was able to take horticulture courses at Cornell University.

Working as an experimental teacher in Loudonville Elementary School, was very rewarding because we did a lot of unusual projects with the students using non-traditional teaching methods. For example, I taught first grade and the next year I taught second grade with the same class.

This method of teaching proved to be very successful, because we got to know the students in a more personal way. As a matter of fact, when I visited the Loudonville Elementary school in 2002 on an outing with the Child's Nursing Home, the teachers there told me they were currently trying this method and they called it "looping"

For women of the future, I would like to share some of the wonderful projects that we accomplished.

We did a unit on carpentry where we used a workbench with a tool board. The tools were specifically marked so the children would know where to put the tools back.

We formed a cooking group where we used a little 1930's stove with electric burners right in the classroom. Every Christmas, we would make homemade candy for the children to take home to their parents. As part of the writing segment, we would write down recipes. Spelling class was done from the hands-on activities we did in the classroom. For Valentines Day, we constructed a simulated post office in a hallway corridor that would have been wasted space. Each child had their own decorated shoebox which was converted into a post office box. All the valentines were distributed into the mailboxes by the "postmaster'. When we were studying about different localities, we build houses out of cartons. Which were similar in style to the children's own homes.

We converted the classroom into a long street with the cartons painted and shaped like houses along the street. On the corners were simulated streetlights. The students were able to learn about house dimensions, how people could add onto a house, how some people would have fences and how some communities would have nice homes with no barriers between them.

For the study of geography, we made one whole side of a room with little tables displaying foreign coins connected with a string up to the mural of the world. As a consequence, the third graders got to know the world much better than the sixth graders, who had learned the traditional way.

After I got married, I chose not to pursue my education any longer. However, I did take courses in life insurance and annuities. I earned the State certificate. My husband had an insurance agency and I worked with him after I got my certificate.

My advice to all women is to experience as much as you can out of life. Don't be content to settle down as a housewife, because there's so much you would be missing. If you are young and you settle down, you can become stagnant. Some people are so complacent, they get married, have children, and they may feel their life is over. You do need to develop a spirit to pursue and experience life.

Sincerely,

Irma E. Judge

Dear_____,

Dorene J. Haizlip was born in 1910 she died in 2001. This letter is a tribute to her life.

It is the never ending love of Nana that made our family strong, her words of understanding when little things went wrong. It was her gentle words that helped to make each problem disappear. It was her giving, sharing and just knowing that she was near.

She was always patient and kind. Her gentle strength and constant love gave us a wonderful closeness. She was the link that gave us pride in our past and faith in our future. It's the way Nana would help and comfort anyone in a kind and caring way.

She was the Minister of Music at the historic Israel African Methodist Episcopal Church for over seventy years. She never missed a Sunday service. In addition to being one of the first African American female musicians in New York's Capital District, she gave free piano lessons to any child who was interested. She gave public as well as private lessons. Her diligence and thought provoking style inspired all her students on to greater heights.

Her home—237 Elm Street—became a safe haven for families in need and was a place where a warm meal was provided for all who entered.

She was a natural beauty. Her hair hung down her spine and was neatly coiffed. She was sharply dressed with a "Girlfriend Hat" to match. Her soft facial features highlighted her Native and African American heritage. Her mannerism always demonstrated a humbleness that any soul would envy. After giving birth to thirteen children, she still maintained her beauty and passed it down to the generations. She was an angel in disguise. As we move forward in this life with her legacy deeply ingrained in our hearts, let us continue to celebrate Nana with fervent cheer and look to the sky for her smile.

Our family is a community and product of her love and we will keep her spirit alive for the generations that will not hear her words, or feel the hugs and kisses we speak of.

We will keep her pictures high so that they may see the kindness in her smile. We will tell our children of her accomplishments so they may be inspired by her ambition and share the stories of the years spent together so they may know how deeply she touched our hearts.

Family let us keep Nana in our hearts and minds as she rests. She was our blessing from God. She was loved so much and is deeply missed.

Flonzina Haizlip Moore & Melissa Brown

Chapter Reflections

One Final Letter

Dear_____,

Thank you for purchasing this book. You are helping other women in so many ways.

First, you are helping to raise funds for food and medicine for women in the Democratic Republic of Congo. These are women, who have been kidnapped, beaten, mutilated, tortured and raped. These are girls, as young as five and women as old as 85 who have been raped during years of civil war. Many of their attackers go unpunished to this day.

By purchasing this book you not only have been made aware of the problem but you can now inform others. Your awareness, put into action guarantees change. These women need your help. They cannot help themselves. But, things can and will change if we women unite. We must use the internet and contact our friends around the world and tell them what's going on. Then, we must put pressure on our elected officials to put pressure on the international community and demand redress for these women.

What's that you say, how can we force another country to treat women with humanity and not as slaves? Let me ask you a question. Were you not looking when the United States government went into Iraq and not only captured Saddam Hussein but also killed his two sons? Remember the Taliban? The United States went into Afghanistan and arrested suspected supporters of that regime, blindfolded them, put them on U-S planes and flew them to Cuba, where they await trial.

If ending violence against women were important to the people in power then something would be done about it. I submit that although we are not in power, we have the power. It is up to women to make known this epidemic of violence against women. Most of us are familiar with domestic violence, but violence against women takes on many forms. There is forced prostitution, honor killings, female genital mutilation, along with the sexual violence in armed conflict that we are seeing in the Congo, Rwanda, and Sierre Leone. Right now Haiti seems on the brink of civil war and rebels are marching on the capital of Port Au Prince. One of the women interviewed spoke of the fear that the soldiers would rape the women. Our Secretary to the United Nations, Kofi Annon says violence against women is perhaps the most shameful human rights violation. It knows no boundaries of geography, culture or wealth. Please, let's lift our voices and use our minds and our great strength of compassion to bring peace to women.

Lastly, your purchase of this book will hopefully remind you that friendship is powerful.

Please read the letters in this book and discuss them with your friends. Then, write your own letters and ask your friends to do the same. Get together, share them and gain strength from one another, then go on and run your race. It's a race that you've been guaranteed to win.

Sincerely,

Elaine Houston

ORDER FORM

THE FRIENDSHIPS BETWEEN WOMEN

PRICE - $19.95

SHIPPING
5.00 (FIRST BOOK)
1.00 EA. ADDITIONAL BOOK

CALL 800-877-2693

MC- VISA-AMERICAN EXPRESS

OR COPY, COMPLETE AND MAIL THIS PAGE TO:

BOYD PRINTING
FRIENDSHIPS BETWEEN WOMEN
49 SHERIDAN AVE.
ALBANY, NY 12210-1413

NAME_____

ADDRESS_____

_____

_____

CREDIT CARD #(MC-Visa-Amex)_____

EXPIRATION DATE_____

SIGNATURE_____

MAKE CHECKS PAYABLE: FRIENDSHIPS BETWEEN WOMEN

Index of Writers

ORDER FORM

THE FRIENDSHIPS BETWEEN WOMEN

PRICE - $19.95

SHIPPING
5.00 (FIRST BOOK)
1.00 EA. ADDITIONAL BOOK

CALL 800-877-2693

MC- VISA-AMERICAN EXPRESS

OR COPY, COMPLETE AND MAIL THIS PAGE TO:

BOYD PRINTING
FRIENDSHIPS BETWEEN WOMEN
49 SHERIDAN AVE.
ALBANY, NY 12210-1413

NAME_____

ADDRESS_____

_____

_____

CREDIT CARD #(MC-Visa-Amex)_____

EXPIRATION DATE_____

SIGNATURE_____

MAKE CHECKS PAYABLE: FRIENDSHIPS BETWEEN WOMEN

ORDER FORM

THE FRIENDSHIPS BETWEEN WOMEN

PRICE - $19.95

SHIPPING
5.00 (FIRST BOOK)
1.00 EA. ADDITIONAL BOOK

CALL 800-877-2693

MC- VISA-AMERICAN EXPRESS

OR COPY, COMPLETE AND MAIL THIS PAGE TO:

BOYD PRINTING
FRIENDSHIPS BETWEEN WOMEN
49 SHERIDAN AVE.
ALBANY, NY 12210-1413

NAME_____

ADDRESS_____

_____

_____

CREDIT CARD #(MC-Visa-Amex)_____

EXPIRATION DATE_____

SIGNATURE_____

MAKE CHECKS PAYABLE: FRIENDSHIPS BETWEEN WOMEN

ORDER FORM

THE FRIENDSHIPS BETWEEN WOMEN

PRICE - $19.95

SHIPPING
5.00 (FIRST BOOK)
1.00 EA. ADDITIONAL BOOK

CALL 800-877-2693

MC- VISA-AMERICAN EXPRESS

OR COPY, COMPLETE AND MAIL THIS PAGE TO:

BOYD PRINTING
FRIENDSHIPS BETWEEN WOMEN
49 SHERIDAN AVE.
ALBANY, NY 12210-1413

NAME_____

ADDRESS_____

_____

_____

CREDIT CARD #(MC-Visa-Amex)_____

EXPIRATION DATE_____

SIGNATURE_____

MAKE CHECKS PAYABLE: FRIENDSHIPS BETWEEN WOMEN